DISCOVER THE
WORLD WIDE
WEB
WITH *YOUR*

Sportster

Second Edition

201 West 103rd Street
Indianapolis, Indiana 46290

International Standard Book Number: 1-57521-135-1

Library of Congress Catalog Card Number: 96-68426

99 98 97 96   4

Interpretation of the printing code: the rightmost double-digit number is the year of the book's printing; the rightmost single-digit, the number of the book's printing. For example, a printing code of 96-1 shows that the first printing of the book occurred in 1996.

Composed in Agaramond and MCPdigital by Macmillan Computer Publishing

Printed in the United States of America

Trademarks

Overview

Contents

By Neil Randall

The World Wide Web: Interface on the Internet

For any number of historical reasons, the Internet has emerged as a huge, rich source of information accessible only via a series of not-so-friendly interfaces. The basic commands for Telnet, FTP, Archie, WAIS, and even e-mail are powerful but unintuitive, and the rapid growth of the Internet's user base has resulted in an increasing number of users who have neither the patience nor the desire to learn the intricacies of these interfaces.

Even those who know them, however, are aware that easier systems can very quickly result in greater productivity, an awareness that has spawned such eminently usable tools as the popular Gopher. But Gopher is limited as an information source by the restrictions of its display; a gopher is primarily a table of contents through which users read or download files—and tables of contents are useful for some but by no means all types of information reservoirs.

Enter the World Wide Web. Conceptualized not long after Gopher, the Web began life as a project designed to distribute scientific information across computer networks in a system known as *hypertext*. The idea was to allow collaborative researchers to present their research complete with text, graphics, illustrations, and ultimately sound, video, and any other means required.

Important ideas within or across publications would be connected by a series of hypertext links (or just *hyperlinks*), much like the information displays made both possible and plentiful through the Macintosh's famous Hypercard program and similar interfaces available on the NeXT, Amiga, X Window, and Microsoft Windows platforms. Users would be able to traverse Internet documents by selecting highlighted items and thereby moving to other, linked documents; and in the case of graphical displays, they would see these documents complete with graphics and other multimedia elements.

The World Wide Web project has made possible the idea of accessible and attractive interfaces on the Internet. Using the Web requires an Internet account and a piece of software known as a World Wide Web client, or browser, and it is the browser's task to display Web documents and allow the selection of hyperlinks by the user.

With a graphical Web browser, you see formatted documents that contain graphics and highlighted hyperlinks. These browsers let you navigate the Internet not by entering commands, but rather by moving the mouse pointer to the desired hyperlink and clicking. Instantly, the World Wide Web software establishes contact with the remote computer and transfers the requested file to your machine, displaying it in your browser as another formatted, hyperlinked document. You can "surf" the Web by hopping from hyperlink to hyperlink without delving deeply into the contents of any particular document, or you can search the Web for specific documents with specific contents, poring over them as you would a book in the library.

But what *is* the World Wide Web? Where did it come from, and why is it so popular and so potentially important? It is clearly a system of both communication and publication, but how does it work and what can we expect in its future?

These are the questions answered briefly in this chapter and the next. More importantly, however, they're questions explored across hundreds of documents on the Web itself, and in magazines, journals, and research reports the world over. The Web is among the most rapidly adopted technological entities of a century that has seen many, and understanding it might be crucial for understanding the next century.

Let's get started.

The Concept of the World Wide Web

The Internet, it is said, is in need of a "killer app." It needs one tool, one program, one application that will take it from being a much-hyped but difficult-to-use linking of computers around the world to being a highly informative, highly usable database and communications tool. The spreadsheet was the killer app for PCs a long time ago, but so far the Net doesn't have one. Some have given "killer app" status to the immensely popular program called Mosaic, but Mosaic still has its difficulties and its limitations. The same holds true for the equally popular Netscape Navigator, which has also been touted as a killer app, and for all the various alternative and commercial Web browsers that have hit the market over the past year. The true killer app of the Internet remains somewhere around the corner, and nobody knows if just *one* killer app can handle the Internet's complexity. Until we have one, we simply won't know.

What the Internet does have, however, is a killer *concept*—and the name of that concept is the World Wide Web. In only a few short years of existence, the Web has captured the imagination of data searchers and information surfers alike. Its popularity isn't difficult to understand: The World Wide Web provides the technology needed to offer a navigable, attractive interface for the Internet's vast sea of resources, in much the same way that the toolbar on a word processor screen obscures the intimidating codes that the program actually consists of. Given the Net's history of nearly impenetrable commands and procedures, and the trend in today's software to hide complexity behind usable interfaces, this capability is essential if the Net is to become a mainstream set of applications.

But it's important to realize that the Web is a *concept*, not a program, not a system, and not even a specific protocol. It might be more accurate, in fact, to call it an interface, but even that wouldn't be quite right. The most accurate terminology might be meta-interface—an interface that incorporates other interfaces—but words with the word *meta* as a prefix went out of favor sometime during the early nineties. Calling it a tool would be far too restrictive, and calling it a set of applications and interfaces would be reasonably accurate but incredibly clumsy. So let's just stick with "concept," because that's as close as we might be able to get.

The Conceptual Makeup of the Web

Calling the Web a *concept*, however, doesn't answer the question of what the World Wide Web actually is. Technically, the Web is nothing more than a distributed hypermedia system, but *distributed hypermedia system* is surely no more understandable a term than *concept* itself.

Right now, though, let's concentrate on defining the World Wide Web, or at least providing a definition that helps understand both its past and its future. To do so, we must turn to the three ideas mentioned above: hypertext, the Internet, and multimedia.

Hypertext is an idea that was introduced way back in the seventies by the sometimes visionary, sometimes flaky, and always provocative Ted Nelson. Hypertext is deceptively simple. A hypertext document is one that provides clearly visible links to other documents; and in a hypertext computer environment, selecting a link in one document moves you directly to the other. Nelson's idea was to link all the world's information in a huge hypertext system. The World Wide Web is closer than any other system so far to accomplishing that idea, even though it remains a long, long way from fulfilling Nelson's vision.

The second system inherent in the Web's design is the Internet. The Internet is a global system of networked computers that allows user-to-user communication and transfer of data files from one machine to any other on the network.

The Net is the basis of the fictional *matrix* or *web* found in the science fiction of such authors as William Gibson and Bruce Sterling, and the basis, as well, of the Clinton administration's much-hyped information superhighway (or, more properly, Global Information Infrastructure). The World Wide Web, in fact, is the closest thing we have now to approximating any of those fictional or semi-fictional technologies.

It's important to note, however, that *the Web as a system does not require the Internet.* In fact, a distributed information system based on the Web can be constructed on *any* local-area or wide-area network, and in fact such systems are being developed all the time.

But the first two words in *World Wide Web* are "world wide," so it makes little sense to talk about the Web without basing it in world-wide networking—and the only (relatively) open (relatively) world-wide network now available is the Internet. As a result, we'll build the Internet into our definition.

Even so, it's useful to keep in mind that the World Wide Web is *not* the Internet. As the focus of popular and media attention moved over the past year and a half from e-mail and newsgroups to the Web and, in particular, Netscape Navigator and Internet Explorer, the perception seemed to emerge that the Web and the Net were synonymous. Today's Web clients can perform FTP, Gopher, and even Usenet access, so it's tempting to see them as the Net's primary interface. But these technologies are in fact separate from the Web itself, even though they're increasingly becoming usable through Web interfaces. Electronic mail remained the biggest hold-out until recently, when Netscape offered an integrated newsreader in its 2.0 version of Netscape Navigator; other Net technologies require proxies and/or gateways to make them work at all. Even the technologies that are included in browsers are usually better accessed through a program dedicated to their use, so it's not even fair to say that the Web is the best means of working with the entire Net. Still, what can't be denied is that the World Wide Web has become the most famous Internet item, and certainly the most popular.

So far, we've looked at hypertext, and we've drawn in the Internet. Good, but not good enough. There's another concept involved as well: *multimedia.*

Although we do not discuss multimedia at great length here, for now let's just say that, as its name suggests, multimedia combines various presentational technologies in an effort to appeal to as many senses as possible. (Actually, the word should be multimedi*um*—like multipart, multisession, multigerm, and multilane—but we'll let the linguists battle over that one.)

Put a bit more simply, multimedia draws on graphics, sound, animation, and video to create a full, rich computing experience. And for the first time, through browsers such as Mosaic, Cello, MacWeb, Netscape Navigator, Viola, and Internet Explorer, the World Wide Web offers a multimedia experience for Internet users.

While certainly in need of further development, the Web already lets information presenters place graphics, sound, and video within a page, and users with a direct, high-speed connection can download them quickly enough to feel as if they're participating in full multimedia. With a 28.8 kbps modem, the download process is much improved; but within the next couple of months, high-speed access should be much more available and affordable. The important point is that the groundwork has been laid.

So what is the Web, then? Let's try this: *The World Wide Web is a convergence of computational concepts for presenting and linking information dispersed across the Internet in an easily accessible way.*

Does this help? Well, maybe. Other definitions of the Web tend to use phrases such as "network information delivery system" and "distributed information system"; but no matter how technically accurate these definitions are, they just don't seem very useful, because every term with them needs an individual definition as well. Arguably, so does the rather vague *concept* in our own definition, but we know enough about the word *concept* not to need a firm definition. *Concept* is uncertain, volatile, and difficult to grasp, but so is the Web itself—not as a definable computer technology, but rather as a combination of its specifications and its uses. Using the term *concept* might seem like an author's unnecessary avoidance, but anything more precise would almost certainly be outdated within months.

In its initial proposal, the Web was simply termed "a hypertext project," but it clearly became more than that. What our new definition attempts to do is explain that the Web is a cleverly designed collection of interesting concepts, and allow for the very real possibility that other concepts will soon merge with it.

In fact, this is already happening. Technologies such as WAIS (Wide Area Information Servers) and Archie (the long-lived search engine) are already being programmed into Web-based search tools, and this means that some of the Internet's techniques are already becoming integrated into the Web's conceptual framework. The most successful technologies are those that make their individual components transparent; in the case of the World Wide Web, this seems to be happening early in its history.

The Web contains the technologies necessary to give the Internet a pretty face. Web browsers that take full advantage of these technologies make the Internet easier to use. It's not hard to see where in the history of computing these two crucial ideas— attractiveness and usability—came from. Essentially, the Web and its browsers have done for the Internet in 1994 what the Macintosh did for the personal computer a decade earlier. There were problems with the first Macs from a technological stand-point, and they were written off as toys by the business and computing communities, but they hung on and thrived on the strength of their interface.

Simply put, people could use Macintoshes easily, and that's something that was never true of the IBM PC or its mainframe predecessors. The Mac hid the difficulties of command-line computing under a bunch of objects you could click on with a funny-shaped thing called a mouse, and in doing so it opened computing to the masses. When Microsoft released Windows 3.0 some years later with its iconic, graphic, point-and-click interface (which had originally been developed by Xerox), the masses indeed took over.

Ten years later, graphical World Wide Web browsers such as Mosaic, Netscape Navigator, Internet Explorer, WinWeb, and MidasWWW offer an interface that has its technological prob-lems, that oversimplifies some important Internet procedures, and that has been called a toy for people who want to glide over the Net rather than delve into it. But just like the Mac, it has thrived because of its interface, and at this time it threatens to overtake all other Internet use, perhaps even the most important Internet tool, electronic mail.

Actually, this comparison between the Mac and the Web isn't quite true, because although the Mac offered just one interface, the Web itself allows all kinds. Its most important interface, however—the graphical, multimedia, point-and-click system offered by Netscape Navigator, Internet Explorer, and others, is attractive for precisely the same reasons as the Mac and Windows. No matter what its detractors might argue, the World Wide Web offers the Internet to the masses, and that's its true power. No longer do people have to master the vagaries of FTP and Archie and WAIS searching (although the Web's own search procedures demand considerable practice themselves), and as the Web fully develops it should fully incorporate e-mail, newsgroups, telnetting, and other technologies.

Different front ends to the Web will compete for our attention—currently we have Netscape Navigator, Internet Explorer, Spry's Mosaic, MacWeb, WinWeb, the GNN Browser (America Online), and others—but the principle will remain the same: Link the information, let the users follow whatever path they choose, and once they reach their destination, let them do with the information whatever they please.

Given all this, it's easy to see why the term "World Wide Web" has become, for many people (including those who actually know better) synonymous with the term "Internet." In fact, it's the potential of the synonymity that makes this book possible in the first place. If you want to master the Internet through the mid- to late nineties, you can't possibly do so without mastering the Web as well. Web sites are popping up everywhere, Web designers and technicians are being hired and deployed, and the Web has even become an add-on for the planet's two most popular word processing packages. Quite literally, it's become unavoidable.

CHAPTER

2

By Neil Randall

Putting It All Together: The World Wide Web

The Web is a by-product of the Internet, created because of the Internet's overwhelming size. There is so much information available across the computers and networks that make up the Internet that finding and actually using the Internet is very, very difficult. We live in an age of information, but keep in mind that information—as its name implies—is *formed.* Having access to huge amounts of information is part of the Internet's charm, but perhaps only a small part; more significant is being able to find, view, and make use of this information. The World Wide Web, more than any other Internet concept, allows this to happen.

The first secret of a good Internet browser is making it possible for the user to navigate the Net without having to know, remember, or write down the lengthy and clumsy addresses and filenames that the Net and UNIX need to operate. The second secret is providing not just links from information source to information source, but links that are contextually related. The third secret is to present information to the readers in a way that they are comfortable with, that allows them to interact with the information, and that truly makes use of the technology—multimedia, integrated applications, response forms, dynamically changing Web pages, and so on.

The Web does all three, and this makes it different from any other browsing technology. Gopher, for example, offers a highly usable system of navigation, but its links are primarily to sites, not to contextually related documents or (as the Web makes possible) specific sections of documents. When you enter a Gopher directory, you see a wide range of possibly important information, but you can spend considerable time searching for exactly the document—and exactly the section of the document—you need. A well-constructed Web-based hypertext document can make all of this seamless, although it must be noted that most Web documents remain far from this ideal.

Through the use of hypertext, the Web can provide access to mountains of information in a very usable way. The primary reason, quite simply, is that the information (or, rather, the links to the information) is provided in a manner with which readers of the language are familiar.

Tables of contents, headings, paragraphs, lists, and graphic elements make up the pages of books, magazines, and newspapers, and these are the essential elements in an HTML (World Wide Web) page. Gopher's limitation is that it is exclusively list-oriented, while FTP's limitation is that it provides not just lists, but lists of obscure filenames.

Both seem computer-ish, and since the release of the Macintosh, "computer-ish" is something computers aren't supposed to be. The Web provides a booklike layer on top of the Net, albeit a book with the less-linear capabilities that hypertext and other computer-ish systems offer, and books with their printed pages remain the most efficient and perhaps the most usable information-presentation system we have in place.

A half-millennium of the printed page is not about to be outdone by 15 years of the scrolling screen, and that's what makes the Web so instantly usable. Its usability will only be enhanced, although its efficiency might not be, as it moves toward integrating the multiple media of print with the multiple media of film and television.

History of the Web

The World Wide Web dates back to March 1989. In that month, Tim Berners-Lee of Geneva's European Particle Physics Laboratory (which is abbreviated as CERN, based on the laboratory's French name) circulated a proposal to develop a "hypertext system" for the purpose of enabling efficient and easy information-sharing among geographically separated teams of researchers in the High Energy Physics community.

The three important components of the proposed system were the following:

- A consistent user interface.

- The ability to incorporate a wide range of technologies and document types.

- Its "universal readership"; that is, anyone sitting anywhere on the network, on a wide variety of different computers, could read the same document as anyone else, and could do so easily.

More than a year later, in October 1990, the project was presented anew, and two months later the World Wide Web project began to take shape. Work began on the first line browser (called WWW), and by the end of 1990 this browser and a browser for the NeXTStep operating system were well on the way. The major principles of hypertext access and the reading of different document types had already been implemented.

In March 1991, two years after the presentation of the original proposal, the WWW line-mode browser saw its first limited network use. Two months later, WWW was made available more extensively at CERN, and the Web was effectively off and running. That summer saw seminars about the Web, and announcements were posted to relevant newsgroups. October 1991 brought the installation of the gateway for WAIS searches (a crucial development for the Web's future as a search as well as a browsing tool), and shortly before the end of 1991 CERN announced the Web to the High Energy Physics community in general.

Essentially, 1992 was a developmental year. The WWW browser was made available via FTP from CERN, and the Web team presented the Web to a variety of organizations and audiences, but it was the software-development efforts of that year that would make it a vitally important time. In January 1993, 50 Web servers were in existence, and at that time the Viola browser was made available for the X Window system. Viola was the early leader in Web browsing technology, offering the first glimpse of the graphical, mouse-based hypertext system originally conceived by the Web proposal.

The Web was on its way. But two other browsers saw daylight at the beginning of 1993, and these proved the most important. CERN's Macintosh browser brought the Mac into the WWW game, and at the same time the Internet community saw its first glimpse of Mosaic. In February 1993, the first alpha version of X Mosaic (Mosaic for X Window) was released by NCSA (the National Center for Supercomputing Applications in Champaign, Illinois); it was developed by Marc Andreessen, whose name ranks behind only Berners-Lee's in media popularity surrounding the Web.

In March of 1993, WWW traffic clocked in at 0.1 percent of total Internet backbone traffic. Six months later, the Web began to demonstrate its potential by expanding to a full one percent of backbone traffic. That tenfold increase became practically the norm for Web access increases, continuing into 1994.

The same tenfold increase was evident in the number of Web servers, which by October 1993 had increased to approximately 500. By the end of 1993, the Web project was beginning to receive technical awards, and articles on the Web and Mosaic (the two were already becoming inextricable) began to appear in publications as prestigious as *The Guardian* and *The New York Times*. By early 1994, in fact, the Web/Mosaic combination had begun to attract the sort of media hype that can both make and break a technology. Nineteen ninety-three also saw the release of Cello, an alternative browser developed by the Legal Information Institute at Cornell University, for users of Microsoft Windows.

Several important developments came in 1994. First, work expanded on the development of "secure" Web access, the kind of security needed if real corporate work were to take place across the

Web, and if users were ever to provide such details as credit card information.

Second, the licensing of Mosaic to commercial developers took hold, and even less-known browsers such as Cello were seeing licensing potential. NCSA's development of Mosaic took a turn with the departure of Andreesen and others to form the Mosaic Communication Corporation (now Netscape Communications Corporation), and the first international World Wide Web conference took place in Geneva.

In July 1994, CERN began to turn over the Web project to a new group called the W3 Organization, a joint venture between CERN and MIT (the Massachusetts Institute of Technology), to develop the Web further. The transition had several purposes, but primary among them was that the project had outgrown—by a long shot—the ability of CERN to deal with it. The Web was obviously becoming the heart of the information-providing function of the Internet, and the responsibility for its development and growth required more resources (both financial and human) than one research laboratory could muster.

Over the course of a few months in 1994 and early 1995, this development venture was transformed into a collection of organizations named The World Wide Web Consortium. Led by Web founder Tim Berners-Lee, the Consortium operates with funding from memberships: Full Members pay $150,000, while Affiliate Members pay a tenth that amount to join. In April 1995, MIT was joined by the French National Institute for Research in Computer Science and Control (INRIA) as co-host of the Consortium. CERN remains an important collaborator.

Accessing the Consortium's Web site (`http://www.w3.org/`) lets you see the organization's official statements.

How the Web Works: HTTP

The most interesting part of the way the Web works is its simplicity. Of course, that might be why it's as powerful as it is. You'd expect a technology like this to have the complexity commensurate with its capabilities, but it doesn't. In fact, as the Web document prepared by CERN (`http://info.cern.ch/hypertext/WWW/Protocols/HTTP/HTTP2.html`) tells us, the transaction takes place in four basic phases, all part of the underlying HTTP (HyperText Transfer Protocol):

- Connection
- Request
- Response
- Close

In the connection phase, the Web client (for example, Mosaic, Netscape, Lynx) attempts to connect with the server. This appears on the status line of most browsers in the form Connecting to HTTP server. If the client can't perform the connection, nothing further happens. Usually, in fact, the connection attempt times out, yielding an explanatory message saying so.

Once the connection to the HTTP server is established, the client sends a request to the server. The request specifies which protocol is being used (including which version of HTTP, if applicable), and it tells the server what object it's looking for and how it wants the server to respond. The protocol can be HTTP, but it can also be FTP, NNTP (Network News Transfer Protocol), Gopher, or WAIS (the Z39.50 protocol). Included in the request is the *method*, which essentially is the client's command to the server. The most common method is *GET*, which is basically a request to retrieve the object in question.

Assuming the server can fulfill the request (it sends error messages if it can't), it then executes the response. You'll see this phase of the transaction in your browser's status line, usually in the form Reading Response. Like the request, the response indicates the protocol being used, and it also offers a *reason line*, which appears on the browser's status line. Depending on your browser, you'll see exactly what is going on at this point, usually represented by a Transferring message.

Finally, the connection is closed.

At this stage, the browser springs into action again. Effectively, it loads and displays the requested data, saves the data to a file, or launches a viewer. If the object is a text file, the browser will display it as a nonhypertext ASCII document. If it's a graphic image (such as a GIF file), the browser will launch the graphics viewer specified in its configuration settings. If it's a sound or video file (AU, WAV, MPEG, or other), the browser will launch a similarly configured player, or if the application is in Java (explained later), it will start an "applet" and run the program within the Web browser. Depending on the type of method specified in the request, the browser might also display a search dialog.

Usually, however, the browser displays an HTML (HyperText Markup Language) document. These documents show the graphics, links, icons, and formatting for which the Web has become so famous.

How the Web Works: HTML

HTML is a simplified derivative of SGML, or Standard Generalized Markup Language, which is a code used to make documents readable across a variety of platforms and software. Like SGML, HTML operates through a series of codes placed within an ASCII (that is, text) document. These codes are translated by a World Wide Web client, such as Netscape, Internet Explorer, NetCruiser, or MacWeb, into specific kinds of formats to be displayed on the screen, and on which the user can (in some cases) act.

These items include links, lists, headings, titles, images, forms, and maps. As you might expect, the longer HTML stays around, the more complex it is becoming. The original HTML allowed only text, and later, inline images (graphics that appear on the document) and various types of lists and link types were added, but not until HTML+ were such elements as fill-in forms and clickable maps possible. Not surprisingly, HTML 3.0 promises even more variety, while Netscape and Microsoft (Internet Explorer) have added "browser-specific" functionality to the extent that HTML might well possess enough features to make serious documentation design possible.

The documents you see on your World Wide Web browser are usually HTML documents. True, the Web can display ASCII files, but they're just plain text files that can be downloaded and opened in any text editor. What makes an HTML file worthwhile is the browser's interpretation of its formatting codes—a link appears as a highlighted item, a list appears with associated bullets or numbers, and a graphic appears as the picture it represents. In other words, the World Wide Web would be nothing without HTML.

But HTML is limited—some would say extremely so. Nothing in HTML even approximates the sophistication of the desktop publishing capabilities of today's word processors, and it's a long, long way from offering the design tools of a desktop publishing package such as PageMaker or QuarkXPress. The Web in its current state is still short of the interest of professional page designers, but with the recent additions of such technology as Shockwave and Java, the Web will not only become a viable medium for professional designers, but one that takes traditional information dissemination to a whole new level.

Accessing the Web

The World Wide Web can be accessed through both direct and indirect Internet connections, and through a variety of clients (browsers). In the following sections, I simply outline the possibilities in a brief explanation of the issues you'll need to consider about Web access.

Indirect and Direct Internet Connections

There are two main types of Internet connection: *indirect* and *direct*. Both types can make use of either modems or existing network cards, and both types range in price from free to very expensive. There are also other ways of describing Net connections (Internet books differ widely on access descriptions), but these two are as effective as any.

The crucial difference between indirect and direct connections is this: With a *direct connection*, your computer is an individual node on the Internet (or, in some cases, a simulated node). With an *indirect connection*, your computer is simply a terminal on a computer or on a network that is itself an individual node on the Internet.

With a direct connection, your computer has its own IP and can be established as a server for FTP, Gopher, News, or the World Wide Web. In turn, you can use software to bring mail and software directly to your computer. Direct access is often necessary if you want to use programs such as Internet Explorer for Windows or Netscape for Macintosh, as well as the other graphical software available for these machines. It is possible to access this software through some other connection tools, such as PC packages that connect to X Window servers, but for many users direct access is the only means available.

With an indirect connection, by contrast, you are given disk space and access time on another computer. When you receive mail, the mail stays on that server, and when you transfer files they are stored on that server as well. (You can download this information to your own computer through a variety of means, but that's a separate activity entirely.) With an indirect connection you can't normally use graphical software such as a Web browser, and instead you must rely on the text-based browsers that your server can run.

Uses of the Web

The Web can be used for multiple purposes. The following sections provide a brief overview of the Web's offerings—from disseminating research and information to providing customer support.

Graphical Design of Information

For a long time, book publishers have known the importance of graphical design. So have computer users—as anyone with a word processor and a set of fonts is well aware. Over networks, however, information has been presented largely as unformatted ASCII, primarily because there were few choices. (ASCII has been an extremely valuable "lowest common denominator," but it is limited.) Exceptions have existed on the Mac, of course, which has had built-in networking since its inception, and more recently on platforms such as NeXTStep, OS/2, and Windows. But over the Internet and other wide area networks, text has been the dominant mode of presentation.

The Web changes that. At least, it changes it if you consider a graphical browser as a default, which is clearly what's happening. Suddenly, information at remote sites can be presented in graphical format, complete with font choices and incorporated drawings, photographs, and other multimedia elements.

The results might have their downside—along the lines of trivial, unnecessary information presented solely because it's possible— but the plus side of the ledger is far more likely. Graphical elements offer different kinds of information, and information providers are researching precisely what that means. We are beginning to see strong uses of charts, diagrams, illustrations, tables, graphics, photographs, maps, flowcharts, and all other kinds of graphical representations as the Web's capabilities increase, and this can only mean an increase in the comprehensibility of the information. Of course, it all has to be done right, but that's another issue. The fact that it's possible means that those who care about their information will figure out how to do it.

This doesn't mean that HTML in its current incarnation allows anything like full graphic design. But as HTML 3.0 moves into full acceptance, and as Web clients begin to display fully formatted word processing and desktop publishing files, it almost undoubtedly will. At that point, we should begin to see exceptionally strong designs.

Dissemination of Research

Dissemination of research was, of course, one of the original purposes of the Internet, and more particularly of the Web project at CERN. Today, the Web is being used for this purpose to a certain degree, but perhaps more importantly—for the sake of its mass acceptance, at least—it's being used to make research findings available to the general public. The sheer amount of research available through diligent Web searching is staggering, and much of it is presented so that it's as easily understandable as possible.

This is an important development. As more publicly funded research agencies are called upon to account for their expenditures and activities, they are being forced to come up with increasingly creative ways of making their work known to the public. But booklets and pamphlets distributed through direct mailings are expensive and usually ignored, so getting the word out is difficult.

What better way than the Web? Through a well-designed HTML page, an organization can now demonstrate its activities graphically and comprehensibly, and these pages can be updated inexpensively and frequently as a means of continuing to foster public interest. Organizations like NASA are making extensive use of this kind of public dissemination, and we can expect others to do so as well. Among other things, it's a way of making research timely, enjoyable, and interactive.

Browsing and Ordering of Products

We're already beginning to see product ordering available through the Web, even though discussions continue as to its security for such activities as credit card use. In the near future, "secure" Mosaic will find a variety of releases, and when that happens, expect to see a flurry of Web shopping centers opening. Until then, you can find a considerable variety of products to order on the Web, ranging from flowers to books to music CDs.

What's the appeal? Very simply, this is home shopping at its most interactive. Unlike home-shopping TV stations, you don't have to sit through 15 descriptions of cubic zirconium rings and bracelets in order to find that elusive Wayne Gretzky undershirt you've been looking for. Shopping on the Web is more like walking into a shopping mall, and in fact *mall* is the name given to many current Web offerings. Just click on the shop you want, turn on the inline graphics to see a picture of the product you're looking for, and then go to the order forms page to do the actual ordering.

Client and Customer Support

The World Wide Web's potential for client and customer support is extremely strong. Already, companies like U.S. Robotics and Digital Equipment Corporation are using the Web to make available to their customers such items as technical documents, software patches, and the answers to frequently asked questions. The benefits of this approach are obvious. Customers with Web access can take care of their own information needs, resulting in less strain on the supplier's support staff and, quite likely, an improved perception of customer service on the customer's part.

The only danger to this approach is the possibility that the Web will be used as a substitute for person-to-person support. But that's not a danger at all if the Web site offers everything the customer needs, and in many cases that might well be true.

Consider, for example, the possibility of Web-based tutorials offering step-by-step installation procedures for a new piece of equipment, or for that matter how to program your VCR. If it's well designed, it will be better than a tech support phone call because it shows, rather than tells, the customer what to do.

Of course, HTML forms can also be used to provide feedback and questions on products, and these can be posted as well. The idea is to have a place where customers can feel they haven't been forgotten, and where they can learn from the experiences of other customers as well. That's what we're starting to see.

Display of Creative Arts

For some reason, people in the creative arts are often perceived as traditionalists, stodgy and resistant to new technologies. Yes, there are some of those. But throughout history artists have been among the first to adopt new technologies to their own purposes, as witnessed by everything from the printing press to MIDI. And there's every indication that the artistic community is seeing the World Wide Web as yet another medium that it can exploit in order to present its work and link up with other artists.

Already we have online galleries featuring new visual art, collaborative artistic efforts of a kind not previously possible, and presentations of artwork that outsiders are asked to evaluate. Examples of creative writing are springing up all over the Web, including some interactive stories and illustrated texts as well. There are even some preliminary attempts at Web-based drama.

The Web offers artists a couple of very important features. First, it allows an inexpensive way of mounting work. As long as the site is in place, the rest is up to the artist, in a way that differs considerably from standard galleries or street corners. Second, everyone posting art on the Web has a built-in global audience, and that's something about which artists can usually only dream. Obviously, there are media that will never be entirely suited to Web presentation, but if today's efforts are any indication the Web, all by itself, could lead to a kind of renaissance in both the amount of artwork publicly available and the ability of a mass audience to access and appreciate it.

The Future of the Web

For any technology, it's impossible to predict the future. No sooner are the predictions made than the technology develops unexpected adherents and unforeseen uses. This was the case with gunpowder, with television, with computers, and now with multimedia, online services, and the Internet itself. But trends count for something, and the Web has revealed nothing if not a series of trends toward future use. Here are some, presented as ideas to be explored.

■ **Full-Scale Publishing**

A wide range of publishers has already appeared on the Web. Some have presented samples of publications; others have presented full texts. In the future, there's every reason to expect full publishing efforts on the Web, everything ranging from children's books through advertising-laden magazines.

■ **Voting**

Well, why not? With fill-in forms establishing themselves as perhaps the most important single advance in Internet-based technology, and with the White House and other governments turning to the Net for information dissemination of a variety of kinds, it seems only a matter of time until the Web can be used for voting—maybe not in a presidential election, at least for a while, but certainly for other purposes. If the idea is to get more people voting on public issues, why not use all public media?

■ **Live Interactive Entertainment**

Yes, we have television. But television is presentation only, not interaction, and here the Web can make a difference. Why not comedy routines in which Web users participate in skits and jokes? Why not dramatic pieces in which Web users influence the outcome? How about real-time role-playing games?

■ **News**

The problem with CNN or any other continual news supply is that the news we get is the news they decide we'll get. Here the Web's possibilities are enormous. How about fully customizable news packages, so that if we want to focus on

Rwanda, or the Middle East, or a flood or earthquake area, or for that matter the qualifying games among African teams for the 1998 World Cup, we can get the text, audio, and video of whatever subject we want. Companies such as Turner Broadcasting, Discovery Channel, Microsoft, and ESPN have already made great inroads into creating information "on demand."

■ **Distance Education**

Obvious, maybe, but no less important for being so. For decades, universities and colleges have been looking for ways of offering courses to students who don't have access to the campus (usually because of physical distance). The Web is beginning to see activity in this regard, and this activity will increase dramatically over the next few years. Watch for full university-level courses to be offered over the Web to all registered students (and perhaps others as well), complete with real-time seminars and exams, and professors' visiting hours.

■ **Distance Presentations**

Organizations with high-speed Internet connections might well consider offering multimedia presentations over the Web. These need not be real-time presentations—which eliminates some of the problems presented by desktop conferencing—and they offer the benefit of eliminating travel and accommodation costs, as well as downtime costs, for presentation attendees. Presentations can take full advantage of the Web's multimedia and networking capabilities, and the HTML pages can be quickly redesigned and updated as a result of the presentation. Another benefit is that the presentation can offer links to other information sources, all of which will be updated by the site being linked. The presentation will thus be always up-to-date.

There are other applications: scheduling, interpersonal communication, meetings and conferences, you name it. But the Web is far from the only technology whose future points toward these possibilities, and it remains to be seen if it will overtake, fall behind, or simply incorporate all the rest. What's certain is that the Web is extremely flexible, and that its capabilities haven't begun to be explored.

By *Dick Oliver and Ned Snell*

Internet Browsers: Internet Explorer and Netscape Navigator

The tool used to access the World Wide Web, or more correctly, the Internet, is called a *browser*. This name stems from the way you can easily browse through many of the documents, files, and services provided by many different types of servers all over the Internet.

In this sense, a Web browser can best be thought of as an Internet client program for all occasions. Built into most browsers is the capability to communicate with FTP servers, Usenet newsgroup servers, and even WAIS or Gopher servers. More importantly, you access all these servers using the same familiar interface. If this were all that the World Wide Web was capable of, it would already be a valuable tool to many people. However, with the addition of its own special type of server, the World Wide Web truly is the Internet navigator.

Hypertext

To assist you as you explore the World Wide Web, its developers adopted the hypertext system as the basis for its navigation environment.

Hypertext is a process that allows special connections or hotlinks to be embedded in the text displayed on the browser's screen. Clicking on one of these links tells the browser to load the document the link points to. With these links, you can very easily move from document to document without ever needing to know the physical name of the document or even its location. You simply click on a word that reads stocks or bobsled and your WWW browser knows where to go to locate this new information.

What's more, these links can also take you to files on FTP sites, newsgroups, and other services offered anywhere on the Internet.

URLs

To make such a system a reality, a new type of addressing system needed to be developed that could describe not only the location of a file or server, but its type. The World Wide Web uses an addressing system known as a Uniform Resource Locator (URL) to achieve this.

A URL consists of four separate parts that, when combined, completely define the location of any file or service located anywhere on the Internet. These parts are the protocol, domain name, path, and filename. A completed URL will usually look something like this: http://home.mcom.com/home/internet-search.html.

The Protocol

The most important part of any URL is the protocol definition. This piece of information defines the type of server the selected link points to. Without this information, the WWW browser doesn't know which port and server it needs to talk to in order to obtain the information pointed to by the selected hotlink. The main protocols are listed in Table 3.1.

Table 3.1. URL protocols.

Protocol	Service
file:	In addition to referencing information located on the Internet, most WWW browsers can also access files stored on your local hard drive. If file: is followed by a ///C¦, this indicates that the URL points to a file on your local C: drive. Otherwise it performs the same function as the ftp: protocol.
ftp:	If the nominated link points to a file stored on an anonymous FTP server, the URL must begin with this definition.
http:	All HTML documents are usually stored on a WWW server. HTTP (Hypertext Transfer Protocol) refers to the protocol used by these servers.
gopher:	All WWW browsers can also navigate their way around a Gopher server by using this protocol definition.
mailto:	This is a special type of URL that lets you send an e-mail message.
news:	Links that point to Usenet newsgroups must be declared using this protocol.
telnet:	To indicate that a link needs to open a telnet session, the URL begins with telnet:. Most WWW browsers can't open a telnet session themselves. Instead, they will usually launch a separate telnet client when such links are selected.
wais:	In theory, all WWW browsers can access WAIS servers, but most users prefer to use WAIS gateways such as WAISgate instead.

Domain Name

Following the protocol definition, the next item of information to be defined by a URL is the location of the server housing the file or information pointed to by the hotlink.

Like all other Internet services, this can be done by using either the domain name of the server or its corresponding IP address. However, the use of IP addresses is frowned upon by most of the WWW community because it does not describe in an easily understandable form the name of the site that the URL refers to.

When the protocol definition and the domain name are combined using the / / symbol, the result is a URL definition that accurately indicates the location and type of server. In addition, due to the nature of the World Wide Web, in most cases you can access a server's home page or root directory by using just these two pieces of information.

For example, the following URL takes you straight to the home page of the U.S. Robotics WWW server without the need for either a path or filename: http://www.usr.com/.

Path and Filename

The last two components of a URL may or may not exist, depending on the location and type of information any given hotlink points to. In most cases, however, you will find that both a path and a filename are listed as a part of the URL.

When describing the path to a file, a URL uses the standard UNIX method for path definitions, separating each directory by a forward slash (/). Windows users should be careful not to fall into the trap of using the DOS backslash (\), because most WWW browsers will fail to understand what you have entered.

Relative Addressing

A special type of URL does not contain a domain name, but may still contain a path and filename.

This type of URL is referred to as a relative address. Instead of supplying a full domain name and path itself, this type of URL adopts the domain name and path of the last URL that the server accessed and looks for the specified file based on this information.

Many WWW servers use this type of addressing to move between pages because it makes for considerably easier site maintenance, especially if a group of pages needs to be relocated to a different server or directory.

WWW Servers

To manage all these hypertext documents, a new type of server and a corresponding communications protocol were developed.

The protocol, known as the Hypertext Transport Protocol (HTTP), lets WWW browsers communicate with special WWW servers that contain collections of hypertext documents called HTML pages. These pages contain the information and links displayed by the WWW browser. There are now thousands of WWW servers in operation all over the world, joined together by the many hotlinks in the over four million HTML pages that provide information as diverse as the Internet itself.

Although HTTP began life as a relatively simple communications protocol, recent developments have seen the addition of new capabilities, including secure transaction layers, firewalls, and proxy servers. All of these enhance the capabilities provided by the World Wide Web. Luckily, there is little need for you to learn about any of the capabilities in order to take advantage of the World Wide Web. For those of you who would like to know more, the best place to start is the HTTP information pages compiled by the W3 consortium at `http://www.w3.org/hypertext/WWW/Protocols/Overview.html`.

Using Microsoft's Internet Explorer 2.0

The first Microsoft Internet Explorer, Internet Explorer 1.0, was released concurrently with Windows 95. Since August of 1995, it has been available for download from the Internet and online services, and is bundled in the Microsoft Plus! add-in package. Version 1.0 is a decent Web browser, and a particularly quick-running one as 32-bit Windows browsers go. However, it's a little short in the feature department in a few important respects.

Unlike its chief competitors, Mosaic and Netscape, the debut version of Internet Explorer lacked support for SMTP—so it could not send e-mail directly from the browser—and NNTP—so it could not access newsgroups. Instead, Internet Explorer 1.0 opened Exchange when an e-mail link was clicked or a `mailto:` URL entered, and it did nothing when you clicked a newsgroup link or entered a news: URL—unless your Internet connection was The Microsoft Network (MSN). In this case, Internet Explorer opened the clunky MSN interface for newsgroup access. Clearly, the initial Internet Explorer was designed principally as a Web browser for MSN accounts (which require Exchange and the MSN interface for e-mail and newsgroups anyway), and was designed only secondarily for Internet accounts supplied through ISPs.

Is Internet Explorer 2.0 better than its predecessor? In a word, yes—the new version includes a number of leading-edge enhancements, described in the following section. Has it overcome its e-mail and newsgroup deficiencies? Surprisingly, not really. Version 2.0 features a rudimentary, read-only newsgroup capability, and still has no built-in e-mail client—like version 1.0, it fires up Exchange when e-mail functions are required.

However, if you are like many Internet users and you are not necessarily intent on using your Web browser for all Internet tasks (and don't mind detouring to mail and newsreader clients when such functions are called for), you may find Internet Explorer 2.0 an especially snappy, powerful choice for fast, full-power Web browsing and state-of-the art handling of advanced media types. Read on...

Neat Stuff in Release 2.0

While some of the enhancements in Internet Explorer 2.0 offer you new, convenient ways to navigate, many don't involve you at all—they're enhancements that allow Internet Explorer 2.0 to take advantage of page formatting, media, security, and communications enhancements in Web documents and their servers.

What follows is a summary of the more important and interesting features of Internet Explorer 2.0. Those that involve operation by you are described in greater detail later in this chapter.

Advanced media handling: Internet Explorer 2.0 supports a number of new online media types enabled by HTML extensions. The most important of these are as follows:

■ Inline video and sounds: Before inline video and sound extensions to HTML, you could not play video and sound clips on the Web automatically when you accessed a page;

the user was required to execute a link to play a video or sound clip. Internet Explorer 2.0 supports recent HTML extensions that allow video (.AVI files) and sound (.WAV, .MID, .AU or .AIF) clips to play automatically as part of a Web page, just as inline graphics appear automatically. Because inline video and sound require a great deal of data transfer and may, therefore, slow down access to pages that feature them, you can switch off Internet Explorer 2.0's inline video or sound support.

■ Scrolling text marquees: Internet Explorer 2.0 can display banners in which text moves like a Times Square marquee. These banners are enabled by new HTML extensions and continue scrolling along, even after you click "stop."

■ Client pull: Internet Explorer 2.0 (the "client") can be instructed by an HTML document to "pull" a sequence of graphics from a Web server to create simple animations.

■ Tables: Internet Explorer 2.0 can display formatted HTML tables (see Figure 3.1).

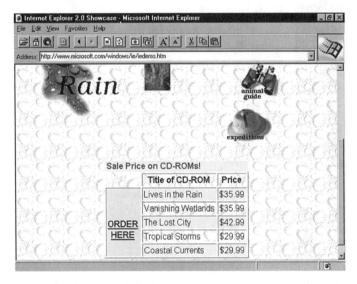

Figure 3.1. *Microsoft's new media demonstration on the Web, showing Internet Explorer 2.0's support for HTML tables (bottom).*

Of course, because these are new capabilities for HTML, compara-
tively few Web pages make use of them at present. Also, be aware
that while "inline video" sounds cool, the reality today is typically
postage stamp-sized video clips lasting under five seconds. (In
Figure 3.1, the tiny square to the right of the word "Rain" is an
inline video clip of Gorillas frolicking.) But as more pages take
advantage of these extensions, and as implementations of them
improve, Internet Explorer 2.0 users will be pre-equipped to see
it all.

Simplified addressing (a.k.a. "Smart URLs"): Internet Explorer
2.0 interprets some Internet addresses "intelligently," according to
Microsoft, in that it can determine the type of server an address
describes without requiring the *scheme*, or protocol, portion of the
URL. You can navigate to an address by entering only the address
itself, not the full URL; for example, to navigate to http://
www.microsoft.com, you need enter only www.microsoft.com in
Internet Explorer 2.0.

Note

Smart URLs work only for those URLs that would
ordinarily include double slashes (//), such as
those beginning in http:// (a Web address),
gopher:// (a Gopher directory), or ftp:// (an
FTP address). URLs beginning in news: and
mailto: are not supported; for such addresses,
you must enter the complete URL.

Also, smart addressing is not 100% accurate. In
some cases, it fails to recognize FTP or Gopher
addresses as such, particularly when ftp or
gopher are not part of the server address itself.
When Internet Explorer cannot determine the
correct protocol, it uses http:// (Web) as the
default.

Security: Internet Explorer 2.0 supports the most widely used
Web security system—SSL (secure sockets layer), an encryption
standard initially implemented only by and for Netscape. SSL
allows secure transmission of sensitive data—particularly credit-

card data exchanged during online purchases—when communicating with an SSL-equipped server. Microsoft and Visa have teamed up to promote their own, rival security system: Secure Transaction Technology (STT), which is not yet widely used. However, Internet Explorer 2.0 has the necessary STT compatibility built in so that it will make secure STT transactions with STT-supporting servers as they emerge.

Context menus: Every element on a Web page now has a Context menu in Internet Explorer 2.0 (see Figure 3.2). You can right-click on a filename to display a Context menu, then choose Download from the menu to download the file. Or you can save on your desktop a copy of any graphic you see on a Web page by right-clicking the graphic to display its context menu, then choosing Copy from the Context menu, and then right-clicking your Windows desktop and choosing Paste.

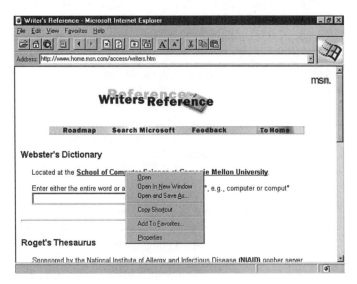

Figure 3.2. *A Context menu in Internet Explorer 2.0.*

Search button: A Search button now appears on the toolbar. (It's a toolbar version of Microsoft's Internet globe icon with a magnifying glass above it.) By default, clicking the Search button opens Microsoft's All-In-One search page, which combines several of the most popular Web search tools under a single interface. But you can change the Search page to any search tool—in fact, to any page—you wish.

Favorites shortcut keys: You can assign shortcut key combinations to Favorites or to any other Internet shortcut. See "Working with Shortcuts" later in this chapter.

Download status indicator: Like its predecessor, Internet Explorer 2.0 is a 32-bit, multitasking, multithreaded Windows 95 application. It assumes, therefore, that you may actually want to multitask—for example, to do something else in Windows while a file downloads in Internet Explorer. To help in such cases, the Internet Explorer icon changes to a download status indicator if you minimize Internet Explorer during downloading. This enables you to keep track of your downloading with minimum intrusion into your other tasks.

Newsgroup support (read-only): Internet Explorer 2.0 can access NNTP servers and retrieve newsgroup articles. Note that Internet Explorer 2.0 allows you to read newsgroup articles, but not to post them.

VRML-readiness: While it does not include native support for the emerging Virtual Reality Modelling Language (which creates in Web pages 3-D "worlds" you can explore in three dimensions using a VRML browser), Internet Explorer 2.0 was built with an extensible architecture to which new capabilities can be added. At this writing, Microsoft has announced plans to release a VRML extension to Internet Explorer 2.0 that will give it full VRML capability.

KeepAlive connections: Typically, each time you retrieve something from the Web—a page, a file, and so forth—the connection between your browser and the server is closed as soon as you finish retrieval. When you access something else from the same server—the next page, for example—the browser must take a few moments to re-establish the connection to the server before retrieving the next item. Through KeepAlive, an enhancement to the HTTP protocol, some servers allow a browser to maintain an open connection between retrievals, to speed up the retrieval of multiple files or pages. Internet Explorer 2.0 supports KeepAlive connections through a feature Microsoft calls Fast Connect.

The next several pages cover configuring Internet Explorer through the tabs in the Options dialog box, which you display by choosing **View** | **Options**.

News

Select the News tab in the Options dialog to identify your NNTP news server to Internet Explorer. Check the checkbox next to Use Internet Explorer to read Internet newsgroups. Then enter the numeric IP address of your Internet provider's news server in the NNTP server address, just as you would in any newsreader client program.

If you are required to enter a username and password to access your provider's NNTP server, check the checkbox next to This server requires authorization, and then enter your User name and Password.

When finished, click OK to return to Internet Explorer, or click another tab to continue configuring options.

Start and Search Pages

The Start page in Internet Explorer is the Web page that Internet Explorer accesses automatically at the beginning of each session and is also the page accessed when you click the Open Start Page toolbar button, which looks like a little house to suggest "home." (Some other browsers actually call their Start pages "home.") The Search page is the page for a Web search engine or directory, such as Yahoo or Lycos, that you wish to access whenever you click the Open Search Page button (the little globe-plus-magnifying glass).

To begin, use Internet Explorer to access the page you want to use as your Start or Search page. With the desired page displayed in Internet Explorer, choose **View** | **Options**, and then click the Start and Search Pages tab.

■ To use the currently displayed Web page as your Start page, make sure Start Page is selected from the drop-down list, and then click Use **Current**. (You can restore the default choice at any time, even offline, by returning to this tab and clicking Use **Default**.)

- To use the currently displayed Web page as your Search page, make sure Search Page is selected from the drop-down list, and then click Use **C**urrent. (You can restore the default choice at any time, even offline, by returning to this tab and clicking Use **D**efault.)

When you are finished, click OK to return to Internet Explorer or click another tab to continue configuring options.

Basic Browsing

With a few valuable exceptions, the basic navigation tools in Internet Explorer work very much like those in other popular browsers. The following section is a quick guide to getting around with Internet Explorer 2.0.

Entering Addresses

With Internet Explorer 2.0, you can enter addresses to which you want to travel in a variety of ways. Use the following action that's most convenient for you:

- Type the complete URL in the Address box and press Enter.

- Choose **F**ile | **O**pen to display the Open Internet Address box and type the complete URL in the Address box and press Enter.

- Click the Open button on the toolbar (the open folder) to display the Open Internet Address box, and then type the complete URL in the Address box and press Enter.

- Do any of the above, but type only the simplified address, also known by Internet Explorer 2.0 as a "Smart URL," instead of the full URL. The simplified address is everything that follows the scheme portion (`http://`, `gopher://`, `ftp://`) of the URL. (Simplified addressing is not supported for `news:` and `mailto:` protocols.)

- Choose **R**un from the Start menu (with Internet Explorer opened *or* closed), type the full URL or simplified address, and press Enter (or click OK).

Activating Links

Move the pointer close enough to the desired link that the arrow pointer changes to a hand with a pointing finger. Click the left mouse button to activate the link.

As an alternative, you can right-click a link to display its content menu, then click **O**pen to execute the link.

Going Backward/Forward

The back arrow on the toolbar moves you back, and the forward arrow moves you forward (available only after you have used Back at least once). You can also operate these navigational tools:

- Go back by pressing the Backspace key.
- Go forward by pressing Shift+Backspace.
- Go back by choosing **View** | **B**ack.
- Go forward by choosing **View** | Forward.

Stopping an Activity in Progress

To stop any data transfer operation underway (an upload or download, a search, retrieving a Web page, retrieving images, video, or sounds, and so on) click the Stop button on the toolbar (the page with an X on it) or choose **View** | Sto**p**.

When you stop during the retrieval of a Web page or its associated media (graphics, video, sounds), whatever portions of the page that were transferred before you clicked Stop remain on your display. You can use any links displayed in the partially transferred page.

To retrieve the complete page after having stopped the retrieval, click the Refresh button (two twisting arrows on a page) or choose **View** | **R**efresh.

Opening the Start Page or Search Page

To open your Start page, click the Start page button on the toolbar (the house) or choose File | Open Start Page.

To open your Search page, click the Search page button on the toolbar (the globe and magnifying glass) or choose File | Open Search Page.

Refreshing a Page

To refresh (retrieve again) the Web page or other Internet data currently displayed on your screen, click the Refresh button (two twisting arrows on a page) or choose **View** | **Refresh**.

Creating and Using Favorites

To create a Favorites shortcut for the current page, click the Add to Favorites button on the toolbar (a collage of a page, a folder with a star on it and a plus sign) or choose **Fa**vorites | **A**dd to Favorites.

Tip

You can create a Favorites shortcut to any link by right-clicking the link to display its context menu, and then choosing **A**dd to Favorites from the context menu.

To navigate to one of your Favorites, choose **Fa**vorites and choose the entry from the menu. Once you accumulate so many entries that they cannot all be shown on the Favorites menu, you may need to reach some entries by choosing **Fa**vorites | **O**pen Favorites, which opens the Favorites folder, shown in Figure 3.3. (Alternatively, you can click the Open Favorites button on the toolbar—a folder with a star on it.) Double-click any item in the Favorites folder to Navigate to that entry. You can also use the Favorites folder to delete unwanted shortcuts or to rearrange your Favorites list.

Within the Favorites folder, you can create new folders and move Favorites shortcuts into them. You can even create folders within folders. To create a folder within the Favorites folder, choose **File** | **Ne**w | **F**older, type a name for the folder, and press Enter. You can then move Favorites shortcuts into the new folder using drag and drop or cut and paste.

Figure 3.3. *The Favorites folder.*

The name of each folder you create appears as a choice on the Favorites menu; choosing the folder there displays a submenu of the folder's contents. Using this approach, you can organize your Favorites shortcuts into folders by topic or any criteria you find useful, then access them more conveniently from the Favorites menu (see Figure 3.4).

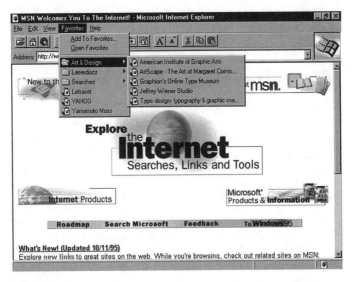

Figure 3.4. *The Favorites menu after Favorites have been arranged in new folders.*

Using History

Internet Explorer 2.0 maintains history two ways:

■ Within a session, Internet Explorer keeps on the File menu a running list of places you've visited during that Internet Explorer session. (Anytime you close Internet Explorer, the history list on the file menu is cleared.) To revisit a place you've been during the same session, choose File and click on the desired entry.

■ Internet Explorer also stores a set of shortcuts for places you've visited in a history folder that is not cleared between sessions, but is always available. The maximum number of shortcuts the history folder can hold is set in the Options dialog, but the default is the last 300 places visited. Once 300 locations are "remembered" as shortcuts in the history folder, Internet Explorer continues adding each new location to the folder, but deletes the oldest shortcut in the folder to make room for it.

From the history file, you can quickly revisit any of the last 300 (or more, if you change the limit) places you've been. Choose **File** | **More History** to open the history folder. Each of the entries is a shortcut. Double-click any entry to navigate there.

Working with Shortcuts

With Internet Explorer installed on your PC, you can create Windows shortcuts to any destination on the Internet—or rather, any computer or document for which an URL can be composed. You can put these shortcuts on your desktop or store them in any folder.

You can create an Internet shortcut several different ways:

■ Create it from scratch: Open the Create Shortcut dialog (see Figure 3.5) from any My Computer window by choosing **File** | **New** | **Shortcut**, or by right-clicking the desktop and choosing New | Shortcut. For a **Command** line, enter the URL you wish to create a shortcut to (you may enter the complete URL or a simplified URL). Click Next and enter a name for the shortcut. Click finish to create the shortcut.

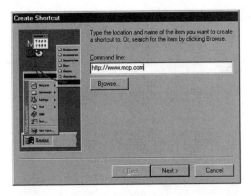

Figure 3.5. *Creating a new Internet shortcut.*

■ Copy it from Favorites or History: All of the entries in your
Favorites folder and History folder are Internet shortcuts.
You can open either folder and move or copy shortcuts
(using drag and drop or cut and paste) to any other folder or
to the desktop.

■ Create it from the current page: You can instantly create a
desktop shortcut to the URL you are currently viewing in
Internet Explorer by dragging the globe-on-page button in
the bottom-right corner of Internet Explorer's window and
dropping it in a folder or on the desktop.

■ Create it from any link: Right-click any link on any Web
page to display the link's context menu, then choose Create
Shortcut.

To see where a shortcut leads, display its Properties sheet. Right-
click the shortcut and choose Properties. Then click the Internet
Shortcut tab (see Figure 3.6) to see the Target URL.

To use an existing shortcut to navigate to an Internet destination,
you can do any of the following things:

■ Double-click it.

■ Drag it and drop it on The Internet shortcut on your
desktop.

■ Drag it and drop it on an open Internet Explorer window.

■ Move or copy it to the Favorites folder, and then choose it
from the Favorites menu in Internet Explorer.

■ Press its Shortcut key combination, if you have defined one for it as described earlier in this section.

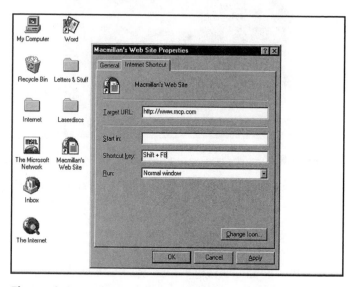

Figure 3.6. *A Properties sheet for an Internet shortcut.*

Tip

The Send Shortcut item on Internet Explorer 2.0's File menu creates an Internet shortcut to the current page, opens Exchange, and embeds the shortcut in the body of a new message. You can use Send Shortcut to conveniently send Internet shortcuts to Windows 95 users who you think might be interested in the page the shortcut leads to.

Browsing Newsgroups Through Internet Explorer

Internet Explorer's newsgroup support is an unfortunate case of too little, too late. In its first release, Internet Explorer had no newsgroup support at all—at a time when both Mosaic and

Netscape Navigator allowed users to both read newsgroup messages and post them. Internet Explorer 2.0 allows you to read newsgroups, but not to contribute to them. It makes you a bystander in the discussion, a Web wallflower. While there are a few garrulous newsgroup ranters whom I would love to see switch to Internet Explorer, I'd otherwise recommend it only to those with only a passing interest in visiting newsgroups and no interest in contributing to them.

Even for reading articles, Internet Explorer's newsgroup access is limited. It does not organize messages into threads, and retrieves only one page of article list at a time (about 20-25 articles). Good newsreaders can retrieve hundreds of article listings at a pop, so you can scroll through them hunting for items of interest. However, for the small number of articles it retrieves at a time, Internet Explorer retrieves not just the headers, but the entire text of the articles. You can sign off of the Internet immediately, and read the articles at your leisure.

Also, weird though it seems, there is a logic to a read-only newsreader function. Newsgroup messages are often called by links found in topical directories and supplied in response to searches. Folks looking for specific information about a subject are likely to come across a newsgroup link or two. All they need or want in such situations is a way to read the article the link refers to, not a way to browse and contribute to newsgroups. In this respect, Internet Explorer's newsgroup support does the job nicely.

> **Note**
> The following instructions are for browsing newsgroups. If you click a link in a Web page that leads to a newsgroup article, you navigate directly to the article without having to perform these steps.

1. To display the list of groups on your NNTP server, click the View List of Newsgroups button on the toolbar, or choose **View** | **List of Newsgroups**. After a few moments, the list appears. Each entry on the list is a link to a newsgroup.

The first time you access the list, Internet Explorer downloads the entire list from the server, which may take a few minutes. From then on, Internet Explorer always retrieves the list quickly from disk, but it also reminds you how old the list is, and tells you to press Refresh if you want to update the list from the server.

2. Scroll through the list to a newsgroup you want to access and click it to display a list of current articles. Each entry in the list is a link to a specific article. Click any article to read it.

Making More of Internet Explorer's News Access

Here are some tips for making Internet Explorer's newsgroup access more powerful and convenient:

- In the group list, right-click any groups that interest you, and then choose Add to Favorites from the context menu. In the future, you can open that group from your Favorites menu and need not bother displaying the group list.

- Similarly, you can create shortcuts to newsgroups to navigate to them quickly.

- Choose Run from the Start menu and enter news:*newsgroupname*. Internet Explorer opens, an Internet connection is established, and Internet Explorer navigates directly to the newsgroup.

- In Internet Explorer, choose **E**dit | **F**ind to perform a text search of the group list (to locate a group related to a certain topic) or of the article list (to find an article with a certain subject or by a certain author).

Sending E-Mail from a Web Page in Internet Explorer

While Internet Explorer lacks its own built-in e-mail client (something that appears in a send-only version in many browsers, and in send/receive mode in a few), Internet Explorer comes preconfigured to open Microsoft Exchange whenever e-mail is called for during a Web session.

That's not as convenient as it sounds; the built-in clients in other browsers are quick, simple utilities, while Exchange is a huge program that may take a long time to open, especially when you're multitasking with Internet Explorer, a hefty program itself. On the plus side, Exchange is full-featured, offering advanced e-mail capabilities left out of the browsers' utilitarian e-mail features.

Tip

If you regularly send e-mail during Web sessions, open Exchange before beginning your Web session and leave it open on your desktop or minimize it. Doing so enables Exchange to spring to life quickly when you want to send e-mail during a Web session.

E-mail addresses often appear as links on Web pages. This is especially true at the bottom of most pages, where the Web-master's e-mail address often appears as a link so you can send comments about his or her masterpiece. E-mail links for communicating with customer service representatives are common on promotional Web pages run by companies.

When an e-mail address appears in a Web page as a link (see Figure 3.7), double-click it. Exchange opens, and a New Message window opens with the e-mail address automatically entered in the To line (see Figure 3.8).

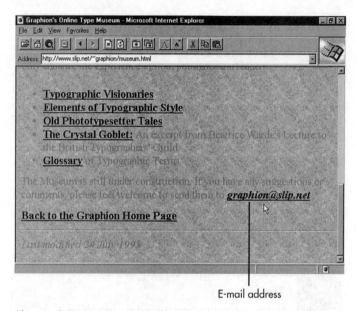

E-mail address

Figure 3.7. *An e-mail address in a Web page.*

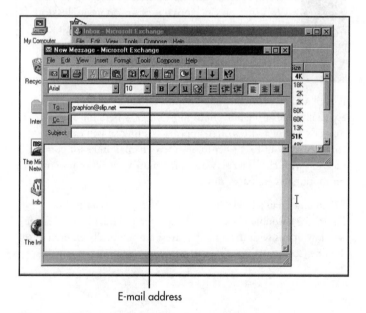

E-mail address

Figure 3.8. *A new message window.*

In Exchange's New Message window, you need enter only a subject line and the message body and click Send (the envelope button on the toolbar). Then switch back to your Internet Explorer session by closing or minimizing Exchange, or by clicking the Internet Explorer button on the Taskbar.

> **Tip**
>
> When an e-mail address appears in a Web page not as a link, but as ordinary text, you can still use it to open Exchange by copying the address from the Web page and pasting it into the address box.
>
> First, type `mailto:` in the Address box. Then highlight the e-mail address in the Web page and click the Copy button on Internet Explorer's toolbar (the double page) or choose **E**dit | **C**opy. Position the edit cursor in the Address box following `mailto:` and click. Then click the Paste button (the brush) or choose **E**dit | **P**aste. Press Enter. Exchange opens, and a New Message window opens with the e-mail address automatically entered in the To line, as shown in Figure 3.8.

> **Note**
>
> For more information about Internet Explorer, pick up *Navigating the Internet with Windows 95, Deluxe Edition,* by Wes Tatters (Sams.net Publishing, 1995).

Netscape Navigator 2.0

When you first install Netscape Navigator, the Netscape home page appears every time you start the program (see Figure 3.9). I strongly recommend that you select Options | General | Appearance and change the Home Page Location to `bookmark.htm` instead. This will bring up your own personal "favorite places" bookmark page whenever you start the program. This page is automatically updated with every new bookmark you add while browsing the Web.

(If your organization or local Internet Service Provider has a standard home page, you could put that under the Home Page Location instead if you wish.)

An example of a bookmark page is shown in Figure 3.10. If you have the Gold edition of Netscape Navigator (or another HTML editor), you might enjoy creating your own colorful home page instead of the convenient but rather dull-looking bookmark.htm file.

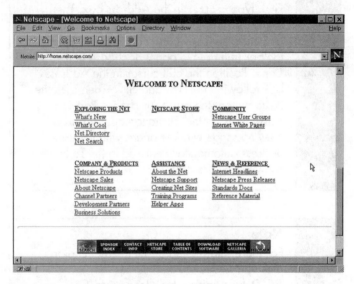

Figure 3.9. *Netscape's home page is always accessible from the Directory menu.*

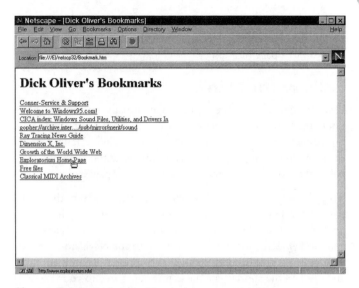

Figure 3.10. *Rather than Netscape's home page, it's better to use the* bookmark.htm *file as your start-up home page. It is automatically updated every time you select Bookmarks/Add Bookmark.*

Entering an Address

If somebody tells you the address of a page that you would like to visit, you can click in the Location box or on the Open button on the toolbar (the icon that looks like an arrow over a keyboard). Then type the address and press Enter. Internet addresses, also called *URLs* or *Uniform Resource Locators,* usually begin with http://, but might also begin with ftp:// or gopher://.

To open a page located on your own computer's hard drive, use an address with *file:///d¦/foldername/filename.htm* where *d* is the drive letter in which the file is located, *foldername* is the name of the folder or directory that the file is in, and *filename.htm* is the name of the file. Web page files usually end in the letters .htm or .html, but you can also open plain text files and most graphics files. Note that there are *three* slashes after the word *file:* but only *two* slashes after http:, ftp:, and gopher:. Also, you should use forward slashes (/) within addresses, even on PCs where backslashes (\) are the norm.

Addresses starting with `mailto:`, `news:`, and `telnet:` are also permissible, but they access communication services rather than take you to a page location.

Follow that Link

Links from one Web page to another are usually indicated by blue underlined text for links that you've never visited and purple underlined text for links that you've already followed (although the color and formatting can vary, some page authors use link colors that coordinate with the images on their pages).

To go from the bookmark page shown in Figure 3.10 to the home page of San Francisco's Exploratorium science museum, for example, you simply point to the words `Exploratorium Home Page` and click the left mouse button. Netscape Navigator automatically contacts the Web server computer in San Francisco and displays the appropriate file as it is transferred to your computer (see Figure 3.11).

The Exploratorium page itself, like almost all Web pages, also contains clickable links. Figure 3.11 shows the result of clicking on `located in the Palace Of Fine Arts`. To get back to the previous page, click on the "Back" (left arrow) button in the upper-left corner of the Netscape window, where the mouse pointer is shown in Figure 3.12. Clicking on the link with your *right* mouse button and selecting **Back** does the same thing.

If you use the Back button to return to a page, you can then use the Forward button (or right-mouse-click Forward command) to follow the same link again. For example, you can flip between the two pages shown in Figures 3.11 and 3.12 by hitting Back, Forward, Back, Forward over and over again.

Tip

Quite often, a page can contain links going back to the pages you just came from. However, using the Back and Forward buttons (or right-mouse-click Back and Forward commands) is faster than clicking on those links because Netscape stores the most recently visited pages in your computer's memory for quick retrieval.

How many pages back does Netscape keep in memory? That depends on the settings in Options | Network | Cache. The more cache memory and disk space you give it, the more pages Netscape can keep on your computer for instant access.

Figure 3.11. *One click can take you anywhere in the world—in this case, San Francisco's Exploratorium.*

Because most Web pages contain more information than will fit on your screen at one time, you'll often need to "scroll down" to read the rest of the page. You scroll down by pressing PageDown on your keyboard or by using the scroll bar on the right side of the Netscape window. Occasionally, you might need to scroll to the left to reveal hidden parts of a particularly large image, but Netscape automatically reformats the text and images to stay within the window whenever it can. In addition, some images are "clickable," meaning that when you click on them, another page appears.

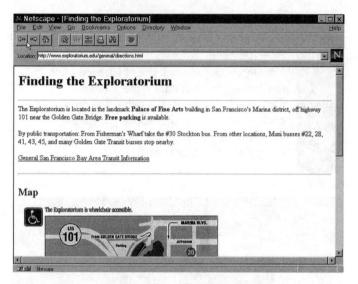

Figure 3.12. *Clicking on* located in the Palace Of Fine Arts *in Figure 3.11 takes you to a page telling you how to get to the Palace of Fine Arts, complete with a map.*

Normally, clickable images that lead to places you've never been have blue borders, and images linked to places you've visited have purple borders. But many Web page authors don't like the colored borders clashing with their images, so they turn off the borders. Also, some images take you to different places depending on exactly where you click. (These images are called *image maps*.) The surest way to tell if an image has a clickable link is to move your mouse pointer over it. If the pointer turns into a hand (instead of an arrow), then clicking on the image will take you to the address that appears in the small status message area at the bottom of the Netscape main window.

Saving Your Place with a Bookmark

You can save the text on your screen onto your hard drive at any time by selecting File | Save As. But if you save everything you encounter on the Internet, your computer will fill up fast! Even if you can store every interesting document in the world, you'll have only a snapshot of the constantly changing Web sites you've visited. It's much more useful and efficient to simply save the titles and addresses of the sites so you can return to them easily whenever you wish. That's what *bookmarks* are for.

When you see a page that you want to check out again at another time, select Bookmarks | Add Bookmark to add it to your personal bookmark list. From then on, it will appear right on the Bookmarks menu.

A handy pull-down menu of bookmarks is great if you visit only a dozen sites on the Web. But even the most nerdy of netizens can find a couple hundred intriguing sites that they imagine they'll have time to visit again someday. When your Bookmark menu gets too long to display, it's time to try out Bookmarks | Go to Bookmarks and explore Netscape's full-featured bookmark list editor (see Figure 3.13). The many ways you can use this editor to organize your bookmark lists are discussed under "Managing Bookmarks," later in this chapter.

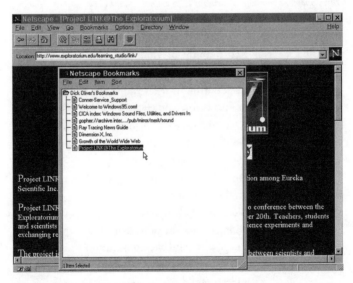

Figure 3.13. *The Bookmarks | Go to Bookmarks command shows you an editable list of all your favorite places.*

Using the Toolbar

You can click your way around the Web without touching a menu choice or toolbar button. But once you get used to using the toolbar, you'll never want to live without it. Though the illustrations in this book show both the toolbar and the Location box, I recommend that you deselect Options | Show Location to hide the Location box for normal use. You can always click on the Open button on the toolbar to enter an address.

Figure 3.14 shows the toolbar with both pictures and text enabled. After you get used to using the toolbar, you'll want to select Options | General | Appearance | Window Styles | Show Toolbar as: | Pictures to reduce the space it takes up on your screen. (If you forget what a button does, you can get a reminder by holding the mouse pointer over it without clicking.)

Figure 3.14. *The Netscape Navigator 2.0 toolbar lets you carry out most common operations with a single mouse click.*

Here's a quick rundown of what each button on the toolbar does.

Back	Return to the previous page displayed.
Forward	This button works only if you've just used the Back button. It takes you to the page you were on just before you clicked the Back button.
Home	Go to the page specified under Options	General	Appearance	Window Style	Start With as your home page location.
Reload	Download and display all the text and images on the current page again.
Images	If you deselect Options	Auto Load Images, no images will be downloaded or displayed on a page until you click this button.
Open	Clicking this button lets you enter an Internet address you'd like to go to.
Print	Print the current page on good, old-fashioned paper.
Find	When you click this button, you can enter a word or phrase, and Netscape will find each place in the current page where it occurs.

| Stop | Stop downloading (or trying to download) a page. |

The Shortcut Menu

Many people use Netscape Navigator for a long time without realizing that they can click with the *right* mouse button on a link or image to bring up a menu of extremely useful commands. Some of these commands are shortcuts to commonly used menu choices, but some can't be accessed any other way. Even savvy users who employ the right-mouse-click menu often don't know some of the powerful timesaving tricks.

Back and Forward Shortcuts

You can click the right mouse button any time to go Back and/or Forward (see Figure 3.15). These shortcuts work exactly the same as the Back and Forward buttons on the toolbar discussed earlier in this chapter and the Go | Back and Go | Forward choices on the main menu bar. Many people find the right-mouse-click alternatives faster to use because they don't have to move the mouse to the top of the screen.

Figure 3.15. *Click with the right mouse button anywhere in the main window to access the Back and Forward shortcuts.*

Link Shortcuts

When you point to an underlined link and click the right mouse button, the pop-up menu gives you several choices for handling the page pointed to by that link. The following lists these choices:

Open this will load and display the page just as if you had clicked on it with the left mouse button.

Add Bookmark for this Link adds the address of the page to your bookmark list, as if you had selected Bookmarks | Add Bookmark from the menu.

New Window with this Link opens a new Netscape window in front of the existing one and displays the page there.

Save this Link As downloads the page to your hard drive without displaying it. This option also be used to download other types of files.

Copy this Link Location copies the address of the page to the clipboard. You can then paste the address into other applications and into the Bookmarks editor or Location box within Netscape.

Internet Shortcut creates an icon on your Windows 95 desktop to automatically start Netscape Navigator and take you straight to this link.

Image Shortcuts

By clicking with the right mouse button on an image, you can pull up a shortcut menu with the following choices enabled:

View this Image displays the image by itself, with no text or other images.

Save this Image as... copies the image to your hard drive and gives it any name you choose.

Copy this Image Location copies the address of the image (not the address of the page it's on, but the address of the actual individual image file itself) to the clipboard. You can then paste it into other applications or into the Bookmarks editor or Location box.

Load this Image works only if you have deselected Options | Auto Load Images. It will load and display the image along with the text on the page and any other images on that page you've previously elected to load.

Internet Shortcut creates an icon on your Windows 95 desktop to automatically start Netscape Navigator and take you straight to *the current Web page* (NOT the particular image file you clicked on!).

If you right-click on an image that is also a link (or an image map), the pop-up menu will have both the link commands and the image commands enabled, as shown in Figure 3.16.

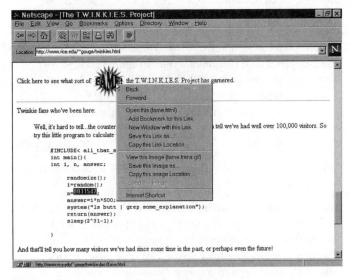

Figure 3.16. *Some images are also links. Clicking on these with the right mouse button enables all the choices on the shortcut menu.*

Tricks for Handling Links and Images

The right-mouse-click shortcut menu can do much more than just save your mouse a trip to the toolbar. It can save you time online (which for most people means money) and can make the information you get from the Internet more complete and easy to digest.

Quickly Downloading Files

Many Web pages offer links to files that can't be viewed by
Netscape directly, such as Windows or Mac programs or com-
pressed archives of data. When you click on a link to such a file,
Netscape Navigator displays the Unknown File Type dialog box,
which asks how you'd like it to deal with the file. When you click
on Save to Disk, the file is downloaded to your hard drive.

The right-click Save this Link shortcut saves a file to your disk
with fewer clicks, but it also lets you save files that *could be*
displayed when you *don't want to* display them. For example,
suppose that you were a Beethoven fan, and you came across the
Classical MIDI Archives (a collection of classical music files
playable on most sound cards). If you have a Helper Application
set up to play MIDI files online, you can simply click on the
Three mov in one sequence link to play the entire Moonlite
Sonata immediately. But you would probably prefer to download
the sonata to your hard drive so that you can play it any time you
like. A right-click on the link lets you Save this Link to disk
without playing it.

Any file—even Web pages themselves—can be saved without
viewing them.

This technique has several advantages over the more commonly
used approach of displaying the page and then selecting File |
Save As from the main menu bar: It's easier, it avoids downloading
any fancy graphics to display if you want only the text information, and it allows you to continue browsing the current page
while downloading another one. Also, long pages like the Classical
MIDI Archives list sometimes won't fit in memory, so Netscape
Navigator actually has to download the page a second time when
you select File | Save As, even if it's already finished downloading
it once to display.

Setting Up Pages for Local Viewing

Downloading Web pages to your hard drive instead of reading
them online can put dollars in your pocket if you pay per-hour
connect charges to your provider or long distance company for
Internet access. However, there are some drawbacks. Most Web
page links use *relative addressing*, which means that they specify

only where one page is located in relation to another. If you download a page to your hard drive, the links on it won't work unless you also download the files they link to.

Another disadvantage to downloading Web pages to your hard drive instead of always viewing them online is that the images and backgrounds won't come along with the Web page without a little extra work.

Pragmatic sorts might be happy with only the text of a Web page; however, if you plan to view a page often enough to download it, you might also want the graphics. Fortunately, you can download those quite easily, too. Just go to the original page online, right-click on the image, select Save This Image As, and accept the default filename offered in the Save As dialog box.

In most cases, if you are careful to put the images in the same directory as the page they go with, the images will display properly when you use File | Open File to display the page from your hard drive. (Occasionally, however, page authors do put the images in separate subdirectories. In those instances, you have to duplicate the same subdirectory names shown on your hard drive.)

There's even a sneaky trick to find out what image the page author used for a background and to put that on your hard drive—even though right-clicking on the background *won't* allow you to save the background image. Here's how:

1. Select View | By Document Source to see the *hypertext* that the author wrote to create the page (see Figure 3.17).

2. Near the beginning, look for the word BACKGROUND= followed by a filename in quotes. That filename is the background image file. You can select it and copy it to the clipboard (in Windows, press Ctrl-Insert), or you can just remember it for a moment.

3. Close the View Source window.

4. Click in the Location box and replace the filename of the document with the filename of the background image. (For example, if the document address is http://www.prs.net/ midi.html and the background image filename is cma-back.jpg, enter **http://www.prs.net/cma-back.jpg** in the Location box.) Press Enter to view the image file.

5. You can now download the image by right-clicking on it and by selecting Save This Image As.

After you've saved the background image and each of the other images on the page, the page should display from your hard drive exactly as it does online. This method isn't failsafe—there are a number of strange things that Web page authors can do on purpose or by accident to make pages display improperly from your hard drive, even when all the images are downloaded. But for the vast majority of pages, you can successfully reproduce the "online look" on your own hard drive.

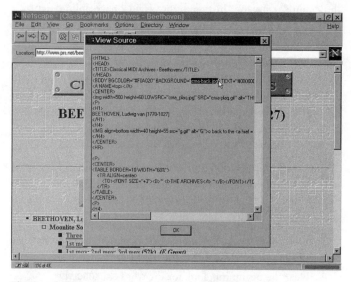

Figure 3.17. *You can use View Source to ferret out the address of a background image.*

The Cache and Temp Folders

You've seen how to save any Web page or image to your own hard drive. You should also be aware that Netscape Navigator saves almost every image you view on your hard drive automatically in its cache directory folder. (The cache is customarily located in the folder named /Netscape/Navigator/Cache.)

If you select Open | File, choose All files (*.*) as the file type, and peek into the cache folder yourself, you'll see a very large number of files with bizarre names like M0obfa12.gif and M0obqa7.jpg. Netscape preserves only the extensions of the original filenames and assigns these cryptic pseudonyms based on when and where the file was accessed. The original names of the files, including their complete Internet URLs, are coded in the file named FAT.DB. Unfortunately, you won't be able to read this file without a special cache management utility.

All is not lost, however. You can still use a graphics program such as the PaintShop Pro to see all the images. The thumbnail Browser feature is especially handy for sorting through the oodles of images in the cache. If you find some files that you forgot to save while online but would still like to keep, you can simply copy them to another directory folder on your hard drive and rename them. Because the files are stored in chronological order by when you first accessed them, you can often guess which files are which by their size and extensions anyway.

If you like the graphical elements in a cool Web site (and you've gotten permission from its author to reuse them), you can quickly download them all simply by surfing through the pages you like and then pulling the last few files out of the cache folder—no need to meticulously right-click on every single button or ferret out the address of the background texture at all!

In case your cache isn't enough of a gold mine, you should also know about another secret hiding place on your hard drive where Navigator stashes files. Every file viewed by an external Helper Application is first transferred to the temporary directory folder on your hard drive and is left there until you exit Netscape Navigator. So even if your Helper App doesn't have a "Save" feature, you can use Windows Explorer or any other file management program to move files anywhere you want to on your hard drive for safe keeping. (Select Options | General Preferences and click on the Apps tab to see the location of your temporary directory.) This method is especially handy for large multimedia files, which would take a long time to download over again with the normal Save command.

Multiple Windows and Frames

When you decide you want to view more than one page at a time, you can open *multiple windows*. The author of a Web site can also organize the pages themselves into multiple views, called *frames*, that pop up automatically. Though the appearance of frames and multiple windows can be quite similar, they work quite differently.

Using Multiple Windows

Perhaps the most often overlooked item on the right-click menu is New Window with this Link. This spawns a new window with its own menu, scroll bars, and the whole works. This new Netscape window can lay on top of the original Netscape window, or you can place them side by side for a full view of both.

This gives you an easy way to keep one main page visible while exploring some of its links. For example, some of the most popular composers on the Classical MIDI Archive list have their own pages. You can keep the main list visible while also looking at the J.S. Bach page by right-clicking on the *J.S.BACH IS IN ITS OWN PAGE* link (see Figure 3.18), then selecting New Window with this Link. By tiling the two windows next to each other, you can scroll through each of them independently (see Figure 3.19).

One of the best uses for multiple windows is to keep an index or table of contents in one window while viewing the pages it refers to in one or more other windows. To keep the index in view, be sure to always click on it with the right mouse button and use New Window with this Link instead of Open this Link.

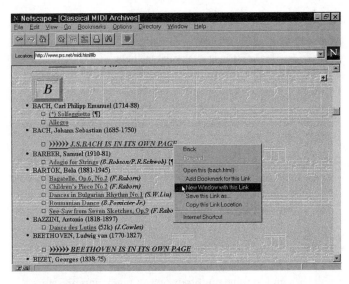

Figure 3.18. *To peek at one page without losing your view of the current one, use New Window with this Link.*

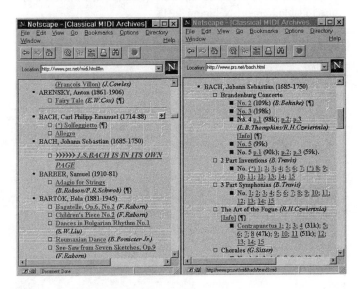

Figure 3.19. *Spawning a new window lets you browse two pages simultaneously.*

Using Frames

When authors and publishers create Web sites, they want to make them as easy for you to view as possible. They realize that most people won't know how (or make the effort) to keep the table of contents in sight by opening multiple windows. Fortunately, Netscape gives those authors a way to automatically create multiple views of a page or set of pages whenever you view them with Navigator 2.0.

These automatic *frames* are not multiple windows—there's only one menu and one toolbar. However, each frame can have its own scroll bar and can be programmed so that clicking on its links can bring up pages in other frames.

Because frames appear and relate to one another automatically, using them is exactly like using any other page. You should just be aware that frames whose contents fit on the screen won't have any scroll bars, and so some multiframe pages might appear at first glance as if they were ordinary, single-frame pages (see Figure 3.20). Other pages might end up with a mixture of scrollable and nonscrollable frames (see Figure 3.21).

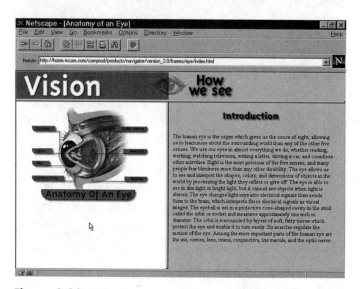

Figure 3.20. *When the contents of all frames fit on the screen, the frames won't have scroll bars.*

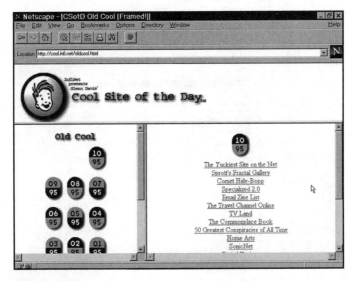

Figure 3.21. *Many sites that use frames combine a "header" with no scroll bars, an "index" on the left, and a "main frame" where the bulk of the information is displayed.*

Managing Bookmarks

While the pundits debate whether the Internet is more like pavement or plumbing, nobody questions the use of the words "document" and "page" to describe the contents of the World Wide Web. So if you think of the Web as a 10,000,000-page book, you might like a few bookmarks to keep your place.

Enter the Netscape Navigator Bookmarks menu. At its simplest, Add Bookmark puts the address of the page you're currently viewing on the bookmark menu for easy access later on. But the savvy surfer can do much, much more with bookmarks.

The Bookmark Editor

For starters, you can select Bookmarks | Go to Bookmarks to use Netscape's built-in bookmark list editor (see Figure 3.22). The editor has its own menu bar with a number of straightforward yet powerful tools for managing multiple nested lists of bookmarks.

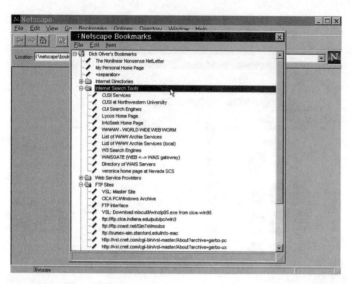

Figure 3.22. *The bookmark editor gives you drag-and-drop filing for Internet addresses.*

To create a new bookmark, select Item | Insert Bookmark. This brings up the Bookmark Properties dialog box, where you can enter a title, address, and optional description to help you remember what the site is all about. To edit the title or description of an existing bookmark, select Item | Properties.

Selecting File | Save As allows you to save a list of bookmarks on your hard drive in HTML Web page format (see Figure 3.23). You can then view that list within Netscape just like any other Web page file—or even add a bookmark pointing to it! To replace the current bookmark list with another list that you previously saved, use File | Open. You can also open *any* Web page file—the bookmark editor will automatically scan through it and list all the links contained in that page. File | Import works just like File | Open except that it adds the bookmarks to the end of the current list.

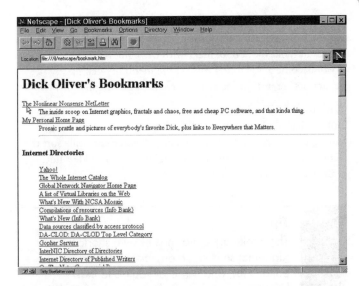

Figure 3.23. *Bookmark files are saved in HTML format, so you can open them as if they were ordinary Web pages.*

The Edit menu lets you Cut, Copy, Paste, or Delete selected bookmarks or folders. (Use your mouse to select one or more items from the list, then select one of these menu choices.) You can also Select All of the bookmarks and folders at once, or Find specific words or letters in the list automatically.

Item | Insert Folder gives you a folder into which bookmarks can be placed. Clicking on the – or + symbol next to the left of a folder opens or closes it. (When a folder is closed, the bookmarks within it are hidden.) To put a bookmark into a folder, just drag its book icon to the folder icon with your mouse and drop it in. Folders can also be placed within other folders, down as many levels as you like, making it practical to organize a very large number of bookmarks into nested groups of meaningful categories.

Only the highest level of folders and bookmarks appears on your bookmark menu. Folders have a black triangle next to them on the menu, and will produce submenus when you click on them. This keeps all your bookmarks at your fingertips without having to open the bookmark editor during navigation.

To create horizontal lines on the menu or Web page (refer to Figure 3.23), select Item | Insert Separator. Within the editor, the result looks like a bookmark with the name <separator>, but it will become a horizontal rule on the menu or Web page. Separators are just for looks and serve no secret higher purpose.

With Item | Sort Bookmarks you can sort all your bookmarks alphabetically. Unfortunately, this currently sorts everything instead of just the selected bookmarks, so you can't easily sort the items within a folder without rearranging all your folders into alphabetical order at the same time.

Tip

The bookmark editor has its own shortcut menu. Right-mouse-click on any bookmark on the editor's list, and it will let you go to that bookmark, create a desktop Internet shortcut (for Windows 95 users only), or edit the bookmark's properties.

Similarly, right-clicking on a folder lets you open and close the folder or create a desktop Internet shortcut to it.

One final feature of the bookmark editor deserves special mention: You can control which folder all new bookmarks will be added to whenever you select Bookmarks | Add Bookmark from the main Netscape menu. Go into the bookmark editor, click on the folder you want to put new bookmarks in, and select Item | Set to New Bookmark Folder from the bookmark editor menu. Similarly, you can choose which folder appears on the main Bookmarks menu by selecting Item | Set to Bookmark Menu Folder from the bookmark editor menu.

SmartMarks

Although Netscape Navigator 2.0's built-in bookmark editor is head and shoulders above the rudimentary bookmark management functions of earlier versions, hardcore web.hounds might want even more flexibility. Netscape has responded to these demands by licensing First Floor Software's SmartMarks program under the official Netscape moniker. You can download an evaluation copy from Netscape's Web site, or purchase SmartMarks along with several other utilities and Plug-Ins in Netscape's PowerPack add-on package.

When you run SmartMarks' installation program, it automatically takes over Netscape Navigator's Bookmarks menu every time Navigator starts up. From then on, when you select Bookmarks | View SmartMarks, you'll see an enhanced bookmark editor.

In addition to a few enhancements to the Netscape Navigator 2.0 bookmark editor, SmartMarks gives you the ability to monitor Web sites for changes. If you have a fast, constant network connection to the Internet, you'll find the automatic monitoring delightful. Those of us with dial-up Internet accounts, however, will be limited to monitoring a half dozen favorite pages when we remember to manually start a monitoring session.

I personally prefer the simplicity of Navigator's built-in editor, even for lists of several hundred bookmarks. But if you want the advanced features and more sophisticated interface that SmartMarks provides, you'll find ample help learning to use them in the excellent online help system. (Unlike Netscape Navigator's help, the SmartMarks help is located on your hard drive instead of a remote Web site.)

Note

For more information about Netscape Navigator, pick up *Netscape 2 Unleashed,* by Dick Oliver, et al. (Sams.net Publishing, 1995).

4

By Neil Randall

The World-Wide Tour

The question is: What would a tour of the World Wide Web consist of? Would it consist of a look at a variety of the possibilities for page design and information presentation? An attempt to show the changes in the look and feel of the Web over time? Or would it simply take a bunch of random Web pages, make sure they look either pretty or rich, and throw them together under the idea of judge-for-yourself?

No. A tour of the World Wide Web should be, quite simply, a tour of the world.

Not an extensive tour. That would take page after page of fascinating description, evaluation, and screen displays, and wouldn't be nearly as enjoyable as doing it yourself in the first place. Instead, this tour should touch on the many nations, people, and designs that make up the Web, focusing not on the technology or the sheer amount of information, but rather on the fact that the Web is, indeed, worldwide.

That's been the exciting part, after all. Yes, there's an unbelievable wealth of resources out there on the Web, just waiting for you to click and claim them; but for the first few years of the Web's existence, watching the Web become a global tool has been truly inspiring. In early 1994, it seemed that every week someone in a new country was providing Web information, and the first click on a hyperlink leading to that country was exciting. If you're just getting started on the Web, that excitement might still be there.

That's why we've chosen the world tour as a starting point. We'll get to business, education, entertainment, and all the other attractions later—because they all have their necessary place. But for now, sit back and pretend it's the first time on the Web—and just grab the mouse and let fly.

The Virtual Tourist

Any time you want to find points on the Web by what country they reside in, Brandon Plewe's Virtual Tourist is a superb place to begin. An immensely popular site practically since the Web first supported clickable graphics, the Tourist (shown in Figure 4.1) consists of a series of imagemaps of the world, the continents, and then the countries. To find your way to sites in various parts of the globe, click the maps where you want to go. For the first few clicks, you'll remain on the server at the University of Buffalo, but before long you'll be elsewhere in the world, marveling at what's out there.

Clicking the European continent on the World map takes you to the European map shown in Figure 4.2. You could have chosen to go anywhere, but Europe is a good starting point for a very particular reason: The World Wide Web had its origins in Europe, at a high-energy physics laboratory called CERN, in Switzerland. So start there (you have to start somewhere), although you won't follow the geographical development of the Web as you tour.

Figure 4.1. *The Virtual Tourist, X Mosaic—*http://
wings.buffalo.edu/world/.

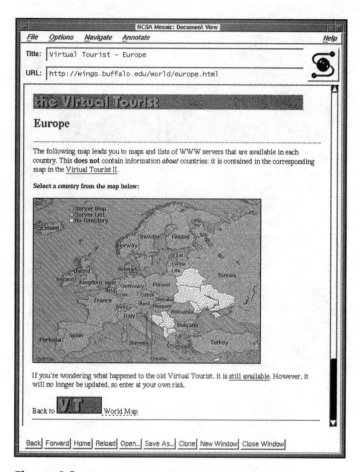

Figure 4.2. *The European map from the Virtual Tourist—*http://
wings.buffalo.edu/world/europe.html.

Switzerland

From this map, it's on to Switzerland. Clicking the country of
Switzerland from the European map retrieves the Web site shown
in Figure 4.3. Yet another imagemap (you won't be seeing all of
these as we do your circumnavigation), this one gives you a
colorful series of links to a host of Swiss Internet sites, most of
which are accessible by scrolling down this long page.

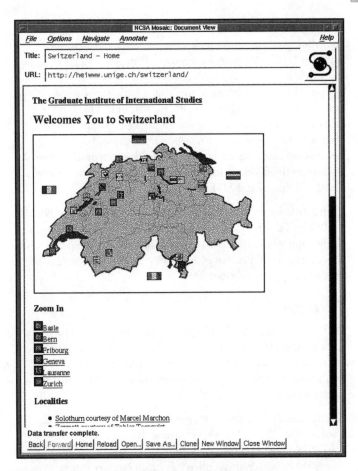

Figure 4.3. *The imagemap for Switzerland, direct from a Swiss computer, X Mosaic*—http://heiwww.unige.ch/switzerland/.

For now, though, scrolling isn't necessary. The Web started at CERN, the European Laboratory for Particle Physics in Geneva, so all you need to do is locate the Geneva site on the map and click directly on it. Doing so takes you to an even smaller scale map, this time of Geneva and its surrounding territory (not shown here), where the first hyperlink is to this laboratory. The URL (Universal Resource Locator, or address) for this page is http://www.cern.ch/; it tells you in the first line that CERN is the birthplace of the World Wide Web.

Moving the cursor to the "birthplace of the World Wide Web" hyperlink gives the cursor a different look (such as a changed arrow in UNIX or a pointing finger in Windows). As soon as the cursor changes shape, you can click the mouse button and activate the link. In more technical terms, you're telling the browser to retrieve the file located at the URL for that link. This process is known by many users as *jumping*. In this case, the link retrieves a page at `http://www.cern.ch/CERN/WorldWideWeb/ WWWandCERN.html` explaining that CERN has practically removed itself from the World Wide Web project, having turned it over to INRIA in France and MIT in the U.S.

Only five hyperlinks are available from this page—one to INRIA itself. Now, this tour is about seeing the world rather than about finding out what's happened to the World Wide Web project, but France isn't a bad place to go next. So why not click the INRIA link and leap across the border?

France

By the language of the links alone, you're now at a computer in France. Actually, you're not actually *at* the computer; you've downloaded a document *from* a French computer. In any case, you've made contact with a French machine, which is what it means to tour the world on the Web.

The language of the links isn't how you know you've reached France. The URL is. Shown just below the toolbar in the Netscape for UNIX browser, the URL reads `http://www.inria.fr`. The `fr` stands for France; you can often tell which country you've connected to by looking at the end of the URL. You'll see several other country codes as you tour.

Note
So far, you've seen two ways to move from country to country. The Virtual Tourist makes this kind of touring obvious, but it's equally possible to find links to Web sites from within Web pages. From this point on, we'll take less

time to get to where we want to go. Instead of moving laboriously from page to page, we'll simply make the leaps and examine the resulting pages. Many of these will be accessed from the Virtual Tourist, which is always a worthwhile place to begin.

Now that you've seen the scholarly side of things, it's time to leave the labs and head out into the France you'd *really* like to visit—the one with the Eiffel Tower and the vineyards. To do so, head back to the Virtual Tourist and work your way through the map of Europe and into the map of France, at http://wings.buffalo. edu/europe.html. From there, click France, and eventually you'll get to the tour of Paris, complete with the Eiffel Tower, at http:/ /www.cnam.fr/louvre/paris/hist/tour-eiffel.html. This is part of an historical tour of Paris, and it leads directly to the famous art museum *Le Louvre*.

Spain

Now head southwest, across the Spanish border to http:// www.uji.es/spain_www.html. This is an impressive page, complete with a 3-D sculpted title, map, and icons. The country code of the URL (es) tells you that you've connected with a Spanish computer; it's obvious how you get from here to anywhere else. Of particular interest are the links to Madrid and Grenada, but others are well worth trying.

United Kingdom

Across the water to the north is the United Kingdom; in particular, you come to Oxford, one of the most renowned locations in the country. The Oxford Information page, available at http:// www.comlab.ox.ac.uk/archive/ox.html, offers all kinds of information about Oxford, the university, and the surrounding territory. Not only can you visit museums and libraries, you can head for the pubs and retrieve a fascinating document called "The Aliens' Guide to Oxford." You could spend hours at this one site alone, but you have other places to visit.

Netherlands

Across the English Channel from the UK, you come to the Netherlands, where the Web was useful as an information tool during the flooding in February 1995. In particular, you'll stop on the west coast, at the home page for Erasmus University in Rotterdam (`http://www.eur.nl/`). The Netherlands has been active on the Internet for a long time, and the number and strength of their resources demonstrate this activity. This particular home page is useful without being spectacular, and there are many such pages across the Web.

Norway

Surfing quickly over the North Sea takes you to Norway, a country that, with the rest of Scandinavia, has been actively involved in Internet activities since the early days. You can travel to The Oslonett Marketplace (`http://www.oslonett.no:80/ html/adv/advertisers.html`), with its host of commercial sponsors—both local and global. A visit to the Norwegian home page is well worth your time, but the glories of Sweden beckon.

Sweden

It's always nice to find a site that won't be out of date immediately, especially when it's well designed and informative. Stockholm has been named (by the European Union) the European cultural capital for 1998, and the city's Webmasters have established a rich, colorful page to detail how it got there and what to expect if you visit (`http://www.sunet.se:80/stockholm/ kultur98/kulturhuvudstad98.html`). If you have no interest in a gorgeous city with superb theater, food, and, well, other attractions, don't bother using this page as a basis for a real-world visit.

Russia

Despite Finland's strength in Internet and World Wide Web activity, we can't visit everywhere. So we'll skip right past the land of the reindeer and into Russia, which is showing Internet activity despite its woeful economic state. The home page for St. Petersburg is at `http://www.spb.su:80/`, and it's complete with commercial sponsorship and, impressively, a Web version of the city's major English language newspaper. Interestingly, the country code for Russia is now ru, but many of its servers still bear the earlier country code, su (Soviet Union).

Germany

Once again skipping over a country with a growing Internet presence (Poland), you come to Germany— in particular, the capital of unified Germany, Berlin (http://www.chemie.fu-berlin.de/adressen/berlin.html). Available from the Berlin home page are links to a number of good graphics files, as well as substantial information about the city's history, politics, and commerce. You can also begin exploring Germany's extensive collection of Web sites from here, many of which are in the German language.

Italy

Working your way down central Europe, you'll find yourself in Italy, where Net and Web activity has been extremely strong. By now you might need some good, solid news, so pick up a newspaper and see what's going on. A typical daily issue of *il manifesto* (which you can see at http://www.mir.it/oggi/) contains the inevitable slightly-smaller-than-readable print. Italian Web activity includes an excellent range of tourist, research, and cultural activity, with many pages—as you might expect—in Italian.

Greece

Across the Adriatic lies Greece, where you'll sail to now (http://www.ntua.gr/local/greece.html). With no time to stop and visit (yeah, right—like you would bypass Greece in real life), let's head on out. Greece isn't exactly swarming with World Wide Web sites, but there's a start. Many countries in the Eastern areas of Europe are in roughly this position.

Turkey

It's not far from Greece to Turkey (as Agamemnon and Achilleus found out a wee while ago), and the two countries are fairly similar as far as their World Wide Web participation is concerned. At http://www.ege.edu.tr:80/Turkiye/Fuar/, you'll find a well-designed information page about Izmir, and there are worthwhile picture tours of the country as well. Interestingly, there's a good selection of material *about* Turkey, especially archaeological documents, in some Australian Web pages, but that's not really what we're after. For other good Turkish material, locate the pages for the Middle East Technical University (METU) as well.

Israel

Also in the Middle East is Israel, where you'll see a significant degree of Internet activity. Although only relatively recent in placing information on the Net, and even more recently on the Web, enough interesting Web sites exist in Israel to make the Web trip more than worthwhile. A top service provider, Macom Networking, operates a server in Jerusalem wherein lies an immensely useful home page (`http://www.macom.co.il/index.html`). From here you can link to the Tel Aviv Museum of Art, the children-oriented Peace in Pictures Project, the Israel Democracy Institute, and if you're into somewhat less significant material, the Israeli Linux Users Web site.

South Africa

Moving way down south, across the equator and into the next hemisphere, in fact, you arrive in South Africa. The country's Internet activity is recent, but there appears to be sufficient Internet access to make an impressive start. Looking at the main page for Cape Town (`http://www.aztec.co.za/aztec/capetown.html`), you'll discover that the city is a contender for the Olympics in 2004. Unfortunately, there's not much else here to see, beyond some very good graphics. What's more useful is the link at the bottom of the page to the Internet provider, Aztec. From there, through a series of audio files, you can even learn to sing the national anthem of South Africa.

Malaysia

It's a long way from South Africa to Malaysia, fully across the Indian Ocean and other waters, but with the help of the Web you can make it in mere minutes, maybe even seconds. You'll land at a Malaysian information page (`http://mimos.my/doc/msia.html`), operated on a Malaysian server by the government. From here you can get a considerable amount of basic information about Malaysia; if you have the patience and the disk space (a quarter megabyte's worth), you can download and listen to the national song. One link takes you to information and pictures about Kuala Lumpur, and other links to further information sources.

Thailand

Just in case you thought High Performance Computing Centers existed only in countries normally associated with a long history of technological bravado, take a look at Thailand's NECTEC (`http://www.nectec.or.th/bureaux/hpcc/home.html`). Here you can find information about computing projects underway in Thailand. If you click the link to NECTEC's home page, you'll find a wide range of additional Web activity in this country, as well as information about its locales.

Korea

Korea has demonstrated a very real strength on the Net in general and the Web in particular recently, and the number of Web sites continues to grow quickly. To get a good sense of what's available, and to see a page kept by someone who cares, fire up the Korean Web information page (`http://ara.kaist.ac.kr/ahmlhs/HTML/Korea/www_in_korea.html`). Not only does this site distinguish between types of organizations and delineates which sites are new, it also uses a distinctive special bullet system to tell you if the site is working well or poorly. The happy face, as you might expect, means things are fine.

Singapore

Singapore has developed an extremely impressive World Wide Web presence. In fact, its famous Singapore Online Guide was one of the first extensive tourist information pages anywhere. With the exception of Australia, this country is probably the best represented of all Pacific area nations on the Web, especially since Japan got off the mark quite late. The Online Museum of Singapore Art and History (`http://www.ncb.gov.sg/nhb/museum.html`), maintained by the government of Singapore, offers a small glimpse of the Web sites in store for you in the country.

Australia

Australia has been a hotbed of Internet activity since the early days of international participation, and remains one of the primary providers of Gopher sites. Their World Wide Web offerings are becoming increasingly impressive as well, and there's no better place to start than the two-designer creation (`http://www.csu.edu.au/education/australia.html`).

China

Despite what you might have heard, Internet activity is alive and reasonably well in China. The Web isn't exactly thriving, but there are some sites worth seeing. Check out `http://www.buct.edu.cn/`, which is especially interesting because of its multiple languages.

Japan

Although Japan came to the Internet community—particularly the World Wide Web community—surprisingly late, its Web contributions over the last year and a half demonstrate that it's in it for the long haul and the big time. The home page for the Center for Global Communications at the International University of Japan (`http://www.glocom.ac.jp:80/index.html`) is a research site that offers extensive information about its activities. This is only one of many Japanese pages, however, and with Netscape and other browsers you can see them in Japanese itself. Stay tuned to Japan, as always, for future Internet activities.

Hawai'i

Obviously, Hawai'i is part of the U.S., but we've given it a separate look for two reasons. First, it's a nice landing spot across the Pacific from Japan. Secondly, and somewhat more significantly, Hawai'i is one of the leaders in Internet activity, with an extensive commitment to state-wide networking and many exciting World Wide Web sites. Head to `http://www.hawaii.edu/News/weather.html`, which shows the Weather and Surf page from the University of Hawai'i (UHINFO), from which you can get infrared graphics downloads and all sorts of information you need to plan a surfing outing.

Chile

From Hawai'i it's off to the southeast coast of South America, where the Chileans have been offering some impressive World Wide Web documents. As you'd expect, most of the pages are not in English—something that will probably become more dominant around the world as the Web proliferates. The home page for Universidad Tecnica Federico Santa Maria in Valparaiso is at `http://www.inf.utfsm.cl/`; from this page you can get information about the university, links to other Chilean Web servers, and a range of other information.

Brazil

The Rio de Janeiro home page in Brazil is located at `http://www.puc-rio.br/english/mapario.html`. Actually, this is the English version of the page, whereas most Web pages coming out of Brazil are in Portuguese. What's interesting here is the level of graphics quality and the degree to which the page is selling the city. Somehow, Rio doesn't seem like a very hard sell, especially since it often snows in April where I live.

Mexico

Mexico got a bit of a slow start in its quest for Internet perfection, but the number of sites is growing continually. Check out `http://www.spin.com.mx/`, which is the home page for a Mexican service provider—which, quite naturally, is in Spanish.

California

It's extremely well known by now that California (with a little help from Utah) is the place where the Internet got its start; so we'll visit the educational institution where the first Internet protocols were put into place. UCLA's Web site (`http://www.ucla.edu/`) has much to offer, including a virtual tour of the campus.

Canada

Canada wasn't far behind the U.S. in developing and sustaining an Internet presence, and it's been equally quick at a World Wide Web presence. There are information maps to the ten provinces and the two territories, while the federal government has implemented a number of programs to hasten Canada's leap into the whole superhighway arena. Many Quebec-based pages are in French, and every province has pages to promote its location and wares. The home page for the government of the Atlantic province of New Brunswick (`http://www.gov.nb.ca/`) has its contents designed as an information binder.

MIT

The world tour concludes with a visit to the Massachusetts Institute of Technology, better known as MIT. Why disembark here? Well, you started at CERN in Switzerland, the birthplace of the World Wide Web, so it makes sense to stop at MIT, where the Web and its founder, Tim Berners-Lee, currently reside. MIT is working with CERN and the European INRIA to develop the Web project beyond its current stages, and currently much of the "official" research is being undertaken and/or supervised from this site. Go to `http://www.w3.org/hypertext/WWW/Consortium/`, the page of information about the consortium; this page includes links to the Laboratory for Computer Science at MIT.

The End

That's it. You started in Switzerland, moved around Europe, went south into Africa and east to Southeast Asia, and then went through China and Japan and across the waters to Hawai'i. From there, you traveled southeast to Chile, came northeast through Rio de Janeiro and then into Mexico, and moved through California and across the North American continent to New Brunswick. You ended where the Web project flourishes, at MIT in the heart of New England.

And you did it all without leaving the computer and the comfy chair you happen to be sitting in. That's the kind of power the World Wide Web offers, and as page designs, connections, and technologies improve further, a journey like this could easily become at least a fraction as good as the real thing. As it is, it's exciting, and it remains fascinating. To connect to computers around the world on any given day of any given week, with very few restrictions and for some very real information, can never be anything less.

CHAPTER 5

By Ned Snell

Using the Internet in the Home Office

It doesn't matter how you define yourself—as a seller, as a buyer, or as a disinterested bystander. As you travel the Internet, one way or another, you move through a commercial environment. Once a public square with the occasional street vendor, the Internet is rapidly becoming a mall—a public place where buying and selling are not absolutely required, but are hard to ignore. The Internet has always offered great resources in support of careers and professions, and you're likely to find on the Net plenty of help with your career. But if you're also entrepreneurially inclined, you may want to know how the Internet doesn't just *assist* business but can actually be a *vehicle* for commerce.

As you may know, the commercialization of the Internet has been its central controversy for the last several years. Much of the die-hard Internet community has been resistant to business uses of the Net, hoping to preserve the Internet as an oasis of commercial-free communication in an overly commercial world. Although the corporate world has used the Internet as an international e-mail backbone and research tool for many years, only recently has the potential of the Net as a place to buy and sell been explored.

This chapter describes how business is done on the Internet. It also lists some good resources that can help you embark on your own online business venture.

> **Note**
>
> The addresses in this section are given in Universal Resource Locator (URL) format. Using a Web browser, enter each address exactly as shown. To use a resource through its specific client (such as a Gopher client, newsreader, and so on) omit the part of the URL up to and including the double slashes (`//`).
>
> For example, to reach the Digital Future Gopher described in this chapter, you use one of the following:
>
> - In a **Web browser**: `gopher://marketplace.com`
> - In a **Gopher client**: `marketplace.com`

How Is the Internet a Business Tool?

The original and still most common business use of the Internet (other than e-mail) is research. Obviously, the wealth of free information available in newsgroups and through Gopher and the Web can be valuable for marketing, acquisitions, product development, regulations research, and many other business research activities. The Internet also offers a wealth of information in support of many different professional disciplines and is also an important source of detailed economic and financial data, both domestic and international. A number of important financial journals are available on the Internet as well (`http://www.yahoo.com/News/Business`).

As the U.S. and other leading industrial nations move deeper into service-based economies, we are finding that *communication* is business. A huge number of business services can be provided almost completely over the computer. If a service can be performed on a computer, it can be marketed to clients everywhere. The Internet provides a communications medium through which clients can send work to distant service providers, and providers can transmit the results back. Such services include the following:

- Financial management and accounting
- Legal services
- Consulting
- Design
- Electronic publishing and other document services
- Research services
- Custom programming services

Although the Internet provides the point-to-point communications vehicle for supplying these services, it may be more significant as a presentation medium for marketing these and other products. In particular, the World Wide Web is shaping up as the perfect electronic billboard: it can show off splashy graphics and multimedia and can offer hyperlinks to expanded information about a company's products and services. As things stand, there is much more advertising on the Net than there is selling. In particular, companies whose product can't really be sold on the Net are nonetheless advertising there for the sheer visibility value. These advertisers include movie studios, television networks, and auto companies.

It's easy to overstate the importance of the Internet as an advertising medium. Although there are millions of potential customers on the Net, their activities are fragmented among thousands of different activities. It's impossible to draw to a Web page the kinds of crowds you can get with a national TV commercial. Then again, a Web page is cheaper than a commercial, and it may grab and hold customers for much longer than the 15 or 30 seconds of exposure a commercial provides.

An important characteristic of the Internet as an advertising (and selling) medium is that it's an inherently *narrowcast* environment. The population is spread among resources defined by area of interest; to advertise, you must lead customers to your message based on their area of interest. There's no accepted way today to "blitz" the Net with broad visibility. On the other hand, the small proportion of Net users you can manage to attract to your ad are a preselected, well-targeted group—something advertisers today pay special-interest magazines top dollar to draw.

The logical extension of Internet advertising is Internet selling. After all, if customers can see a picture of your product on the Web, and read about it through a hyperlink to a product description, why shouldn't they be able to order it right then, when the electronic pitch is burning a hole in their pockets? Unfortunately, online sales is a real sticking point of online business.

As it stands, the Internet is simply not a very secure place for people to send others their credit card numbers or bank account information—currently, the only two means of performing online transactions. Similar transactions made today over the telephone are a major source of fraud, which is why businesses are approaching online sales very cautiously—and with good reason.

It wouldn't be very difficult for a "cracker" or an unscrupulous system administrator to harvest credit card information from online transactions moving through the Net, make his or her own purchases using stolen credit card information, and then cover his or her tracks before anyone knew what happened. For their parts, VISA and MasterCard each maintain a Web site to show how credit cards can be used and what's being done to make credit card transactions more secure. These sites also offer consumer services, such as maps of ATM locations.

One good way to learn about companies doing business on the Net is through CommerceNet, a consortium of companies dedicated to exploring the Net's commercial potential. These advertisers' Web pages can be reached directly, of course, but CommerceNet maintains a page of links to them to help you find them all. CommerceNet's home page (see Figure 5.1) also includes information about the CommerceNet project and good general information about doing business on the Web.

Figure 5.1. *CommerceNet's Web page at* http://www.commerce.net.

> **Note**
>
> CommerceNet is not the only engine to which companies have hitched their cars. Another, the Internet Mall, also maintains a list of links to Internet sellers. Bear in mind, however, that selling can be done anywhere on the Web and in other Internet resources, so long as it is done using accepted practices.

The Internet itself is also a publishing medium. There are many newspapers and magazines published on the Web, many of them online versions of publications that are also printed. Recently, science magazine *Omni* pointed the way by announcing it would retire its print version and move the whole operation onto the Web.

The Open Question: Security

Security is a concern for all uses of the Internet, but online financial transactions are a particular problem. There have been several highly publicized cases of online fraud and computer-based theft and espionage. This problem has done more than discourage the adoption of online sales and ordering.

It has also prevented any widescale adoption of the Internet as a backbone for business-to-business transactions such as electronic funds transfers. Many such transactions are performed electronically today, but nearly all are performed over more secure—and more expensive—private communications networks. The banks don't trust the Internet with their money, and neither do large corporations. Think about that before you type your VISA number on a Web page.

Although high-level security systems are required for overall Internet security, two initiatives are underway to make credit card transactions on the Web more secure to encourage online sales. The first, already in use, is Secure Sockets Layer (SSL), developed by Netscape Communications, developer of the Netscape Navigator Web browser. SSL has been endorsed by Microsoft, IBM, and other major companies, and is the security system for a Web shopping center called marketplaceMCI (`http://` `www.marketplace.internetMCI.com/marketplace`), operated by MCI, the same company that keeps calling you to ask whether you're happy with your current long-distance service. The other Web-based security system, yet to debut, is called Secure HTTP and is championed by CommerceNet. At this writing, the jury is still out on both systems.

Until an effective security system is developed for protecting credit-card transactions, the Internet will be a dicey place to sell. Whether that's a reason to stay away or jump right in depends on the type of businessperson you are.

The Do's and Don'ts of Net Commerce

The basic rule for Internet business ventures is passivity—let the buyers come to you, don't reach out and grab them. That philosophy runs counter to everything today's aggressive, competitive businesspeople have been weaned on, but for now, it's the best approach. In a famous case a few years ago, a Phoenix law firm cross-posted an ad to thousands of newsgroups, hoping to drum up some customers. Internet users flamed the firm by e-mail so severely that the law firm's Internet provider had to cut off the firm's account.

A Web page is a great place to advertise, not only because of the sexy ways you can use it to show off your product but also because you can't snare users—any user who navigates to your Web page *wants* to be there. You can post gentle announcements about the existence of the Web page in newsgroups and mailing lists whose topics relate directly to your product or service. Don't advertise in your announcement—simply let people know where your Web page is (or your e-mail address if you're not using the Web), and save the pitch for when they arrive. Obviously, if you want them to come, you have to offer a carrot to get them there—cool video or sound clips, an online game, and so on.

Another good technique for passive advertising is to sponsor something non-commercial and build a Web page for your sponsoree that also happens to promote your company. For example, laser disc maker Voyager Co. sponsors a number of cultural events, including the Nuyorican Cafe, a project promoting Latino poetry and concerts by performance artist Laurie Anderson. Folks are drawn to Voyager's Web site to learn about the Cafe, and while there, discover links to information about Voyager products and services (http://voyagerco.com).

The Bottom Line: Getting Started

Here's the bottom line: You can advertise, market, and sell anything on the Internet. And if your product or service can be coded into a computer file and sent over a wire, you can even provide it over the Internet. Today, the Internet is unlikely to make you rich. But success depends on being in the right place at the right time; within a few years, the Internet may well be the right place. If you get started today, you'll be there when it happens.

To get started, think about the type of product or service you supply (or want to supply) and how the Internet can play a role. Check out the rest of this chapter for some great sources offering good starting points and other business-related information.

Internet Professional Resources

The Internet offers journals, job openings, peer networking opportunities, and other resources for every profession imaginable. Perhaps the best way to locate resources about your profession is to do a Web search using the name of your professional area (medicine, law, design, and so on) as a search term.

It's impossible to adequately show the breadth of professional resources available on the Internet. But the following few examples may give you an idea.

- **The American Institute of Graphic Arts** (http://www.dol.com/Root/org/AIGA/AIGAlink.html)

  A great starting place for professional designers and illustrators.

- **The Engineer's Club** (http://www.engineers.com/tec.html)

  The place where the slide-rule set hangs out.

- **The Midwifery Page** (http://www.csv.warwick.ac.uk:8000/midwifery.html)

  Links and resources for professional midwives and other childbirth professionals.

Job Hunting

Yes, you can find a job on the Internet—although the jury's out on whether the Internet is really an effective job hunting/recruiting tool. The Internet population is so large and spread out and most recruiters look for a few local people. Still, the want ads are there, and the Internet is as good a place as any to start.

Probably the best way to find a job online is to locate a resource related to that job and then look for job listings. For example, many of the U.S. government's Web pages feature a link that lists jobs in the department or agency to which the page pertains. You may find job listings at specific companies available from a link on the companies' home pages.

There are also more general job listings available. For example, the Job Search page, available at http://www.adnetsol.com/jsearch/

`jshome1.html`, is a searchable database of over 40,000 jobs in Southern California.

Internet Business Resources

This section describes places to find business information and support services on the Internet.

First, you may want to see a list of links to companies already doing business on the Net. Try the Yahoo directory at `http://www.yahoo.com/Business/Corporations`.

Starting an Internet Business

- **Internet Plaza** (`http://plaza.xor.com/plaza/index.html`)

  Internet Plaza offers a range of business services to help companies get started in online business.

- **Digital Future** (`gopher://marketplace.com`)

  An online newsletter about Internet-based commerce.

- **Internet Business Center** (`http://www.tig.com/ibc`)

  A Web server specializing in providing information about business uses of the Internet.

- **Commercial Use Strategies Home Page** (`http://www.netrex.com/business/usage.html`)

  More strategies and tips for online businesses.

- **Small Business Administration** (`http://www.sbaonline.sba.gov`)

  A Web page for the U.S. Small Business Administration, created to help new and existing small businesses compete. Includes business development services and links to other resources.

- **Open Market Commercial Sites Index** (`http://www.directory.net`)

  A pile of links to economic information, such as the files of the Financial Services Technology Consortium and the customer support pages of major corporations. A great place for ideas.

Economic/Financial Data

■ **Financial Economics Network** (http://www.crimson.com/ fen)

Created by the editor of the *Journal of Financial Economics*, this home page features abstracts of forthcoming papers and articles and also includes listings of jobs and job-seekers in the field.

■ **QuoteCom** (http://www.quote.com)

QuoteCom displays stock quotes (delayed 15 minutes), plus a wealth of information from newswires, market data, and more.

Advertising

■ **Chiat/Day Idea Factory** (http://www.chiatday.com/ factory)

Chiat/Day is a former ad agency (now specializing in "brand promotion") whose Web site, a "virtual office," shows off splendidly what a little imagination can do on the Web. Whether you do business with Chiat/Day or not, the company's Web pages are a guide to the possibilities.

■ *Advertising Age* (http://www.adage.com)

The venerable advertising magazine and sourcebook, now in an online version.

Note

For more information about Internet business, pick up *The Internet Business Guide*, Second Edition, by Rosilind Resnick and Dave Taylor (Sams.net Publishing, 1995).

CHAPTER 6

By Ned Snell

Using the Internet for Education

After human teachers, the Internet would represent the most important educational resource in the world if every student had a computer. That not being the case, the Internet as it stands is an exercise in the expansion of inequality. By and large, the students who now have access to the Internet already have access to well-supported schools, well-paid teachers, and well-stocked libraries. Students who don't have access to computers or the Internet often don't have much else, either.

The problem of getting classrooms online is exacerbated by the presence of board members, administrators, and teachers who don't recognize that the educational value of computers and online communications far exceeds the cost. Scare headlines and misinformation regarding the presence of pornography on the Internet (see Chapter 7, "Using the Internet for Family Fun") provide the anti-computer contingent with the ammunition to keep classrooms offline.

However, by familiarizing themselves with the educational resources the Internet offers, teachers, administrators, and parents may acquire the ammunition they need to sell their schools on the necessity of classroom computing. Also, even if that effort should fail, there are resources on the Internet designed to help teachers become better teachers—even when they cannot offer their students the benefits of an online community. Teachers can use college computer systems or home computers and individual Internet accounts to educate themselves and then bring the benefits of the Internet to their students by proxy.

This chapter identifies Internet resources that can be particularly valuable to teachers, students, and others with an interest in education. As you discover these resources, keep in mind that the *entire* Internet—not just the education-specific resources—offers value to teachers and students. Newsgroups, IRC channels, Gopher menus, and Web pages can offer access to a world of information about, and exchange with, other cultures and communities and experts in every field. It's the best all-around encyclopedia, textbook, and teaching video money can buy.

Good Starting Points for Teachers

The resources listed below are good places to learn about how the Internet is already applied in education.

> **Note**
>
> Most of the addresses in this chapter are in Universal Resource Locator (URL) format (any exceptions are noted as they come up). Using a Web browser, enter each address exactly as shown to access the resource.
>
> To use a resource through its specific client (a newsreader, Gopher client, and so on), omit the part of the URL up to and including the double slashes (//); for newsgroups, omit the characters *news:* at the start of the address.

■ **AskERIC** (http://ericir.syr.edu)

AskERIC is a venerable educator's resource of the Educational Resources Information Center (ERIC), long available through Telnet and now available on the Web. It features extensive holdings of federally funded education information.

■ **Center for Excellence in Education** (http://rsi.cee.org)

Information about programs for keeping U.S. students competitive in science and technology; also has information on other education initiatives.

■ **Educational Online Sources** (http://netspace.students. brown.edu/eos1)

Links to all kinds of educational resources all over the Net, courtesy of Brown University.

■ **World Lecture Hall** (http://www.utexas.edu:80/world/ instruction)

A collection of materials about using the Web as a teaching tool. Resources include course syllabi, notes, textbooks, and more.

■ **Galaxy Education** (http://galaxy.einet.net/galaxy/ Social-Sciences/Education.html)

Materials and pointers to educational resources.

■ **Educational Technology** (http://tecfa.unige.ch/info-edu-comp.html)

Education-related links in the World Wide Web Virtual Library.

■ **CoVis: Learning through Collaborative Visualization** (http://www.covis.nwu.edu)

A project at Northwestern University to explore the unique ways the Web can be used in teaching applications.

■ **Teacher Education** (http://curry.edschool. virginia.edu/teis)

A service of the Society for Technology and Teacher Education, this site contains documents and links to teacher educational resources.

■ **U.S. Department of Education** (http://www.ed.gov)

At this writing, Congress is considering a proposal to abolish the Department of Education. But for as long as it survives, you'll find information about its programs here.

K-12 Resources

The resources listed here may be useful in K through 12 class-rooms. They also serve as models for programs teachers can create themselves.

■ **Empire Internet Schoolhouse** (gopher://nysernet.org:3000/11)

A rich set of documents and links to K-12 resources, projects, and discussion groups.

■ **Exploratorium** (http://www.exploratorium.edu)

Hundreds of interactive exhibits about science, art, and human perception (see Figure 6.1).

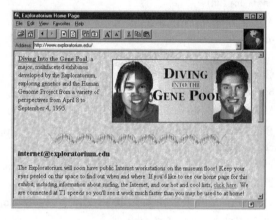

Figure 6.1. *The Exploratorium home page.*

■ **Travels with Samantha** (http://www-swiss.ai.mit.edu/samantha/travels-with-samantha.html)

Travels with Samantha is a travel show on the Internet that takes students to interesting destinations all over North America.

■ **The Jason Project** (http://seawifs.gsfc.nasa.gov/scripts/JASON.html)

A collaborative effort of NASA and scientists to provide an interactive learning environment about science. Jason takes students to the rain forest, outer space, and much more; it's an excellent showcase for the potential of Web-based teaching.

■ **NASA** (http://www.nasa.gov)

Documents, graphics, and links to an array of space-related resources, including a K–12 education program.

■ **Children's Literature Web Guide** (http://www.ucalgary. ca/~dkbrown/index.html)

Provides abstracts and other information about winners of the Newbery and Caldecott medals for children's literature, plus the Publishers Weekly Children's Bestsellers list.

■ **The Smithsonian Natural History Gopher** (gopher:// nmnhgoph.si.edu)

Offers a treasure of news and information about projects underway at the Smithsonian, divided by natural history disciplines. This Gopher also offers links to other natural history Gophers.

■ **The White House** (http://www.whitehouse.gov)

Pictures of White House interiors, access to speeches, press releases, and other documents, and personal information about the First Family, right down to Socks the cat.

■ **CapWeb** (http://policy.net)

Unofficial information about events on Capitol Hill, including documents of pending legislation.

■ **The Cornell Theory Center Math and Science Gateway** (http://www.tc.cornell.edu:80/Edu/MathSciGateway)

A great clearinghouse of sorts, containing links to dozens of math and science education-related Internet resources for grades K–12.

Post-Secondary Resources

The resources listed here can be of special interest to college students—or those heading for college.

■ **Money for College Directory** (http://www. studentservices.com/mfc)

This page offers a searchable database of thousands of scholarships, grants, and special loans to help students locate all the financial resources for which they may be eligible.

■ **IRC Language Channels**

On Internet Relay Chat (IRC) servers, a number of Chat channels conduct conversations in a language other than English. These channels are great places for college students (and teachers) to practice their foreign language conversation skills. Chat channels named after a country (channel #spain or #france, for example) generally conduct the chat in the native language of that country. Channels named after a language (#espanol or #francais, for example) also converse in the native tongue.

Note that there are no URLs for IRC channels. The channels described here are accessed through an IRC client.

■ **CNU Online** (http://cnuonline.cnu.edu)

A project of Christopher Newport University (CNU), CNU Online offers credit-bearing courses from CNU—plus links to credit-bearing online courses at other universities—to allow students to acquire a bachelor's degree online. CNU Online is still under construction, but you can check it out to see what courses and degrees are currently offered, or will be offered.

> **Note**
>
> For more information, read *Education on the Internet*, Second Edition, by Jill Ellsworth and Dave Taylor (Sams.net Publishing, 1995).

By Ned Snell

Using the Internet for Family Fun

The Internet was not created as a playground, but it's certainly made up for lost time in recent years. The amount of sheer, pointless fun that can be had on the Net has grown more quickly than any other type of activity. That's likely to continue as the Internet completes its transition from research tool to all-purpose information service.

In this chapter, you discover some of the many pointless (or semi-pointless) diversions the Internet has to offer. But first, a serious note about a cultural controversy…

Is the Internet Fit for Family Consumption?

It's impossible to discuss the Internet as a playground without first addressing the very real concerns people have about whether the Net is a safe, appropriate place for children—or for adults, for that matter. Stories about online pornography, Net-cruising pedophiles, hate groups, and addictions to being online have aroused concerns among those wondering whether they or their children are really safe in cyberspace.

The fair and simple answer is *no*. It's important to remember that the Internet is not a product controlled by its owner, as other online services may be. It's simply a vehicle through which millions communicate freely and openly. The overwhelming majority of those who go online do so for wholesome reasons; it's almost impossible to come across pornography, hate speeches, or other unsavory ideas unless you go looking for them. But such ideas are indeed expressed on the Internet, as are erotic (or pornographic) writing, pictures, and discussions; hateful tirades against every imaginable group; kinky chat channels; and more. Also, as recent cautionary books have observed, people can get hooked on the Internet—*so* hooked that they hang out online to the exclusion of other, more important pursuits.

Ultimately, every parent—and every person—must decide for himself or herself whether the benefits of the Internet are worth its risks. I think the risks are small and the rewards great, so it's an easy question for me. I also recognize that, even if I were to prevent my children from using the Internet, my wife and I would still have to supervise their activities, teach them to be appropriately wary of strangers, and help them develop good judgment about ideas to which they are exposed. These life skills are as necessary on the street as they are on the Internet—probably more so.

The Internet does not expose me or my family to any new dangers. It merely reflects the dangers of the society at large. Because my kids will have to learn how to live with those dangers anyway, I'll choose to let them enjoy—and learn from—the world online, with their parents' guidance to protect them.

Tip

If you doubt the potential value of cyberspace to families, check out Helping Your Children Learn To Read, a Web facility set up by the U.S. Department of Education to provide parents with online tools for teaching reading.

The page takes parents from exercises designed to get infants off to the right start all the way to fun reading exercises children can perform themselves. You'll find Helping Your Children Learn To Read at the following URL: `http://www.ed.gov/pubs/parents/Reading/index.html`

Internet Pastimes

Tip

The following pages offer a selection of Internet diversions. However, the resources listed can only scratch the surface of what's available. One good way to hunt down new, fun resources is through the Yahoo directory at `http://www.yahoo.com`.

The following pages describe starting points and specific sites you or your family may want to visit for the heck of it.

Note

Most of the addresses in this chapter are in Universal Resource Locator (URL) format (any exceptions are noted as they come up). Using a Web browser, enter each address exactly as shown to access the resource.

To use a resource through its specific client (a newsreader, Gopher client, and so on), omit the part of the URL up to and including the double slashes (`//`); for newsgroups, omit the characters *news:* at the start of the address.

Shopping

■ **Internet Shopping Network** (http://shop.internet.net)

Owned by TV's Home Shopping Network, the ISN is one of the first Web-based marketplaces. You can shop the catalogs of major mail-order houses and place orders online. Note that the opening page of the Shopping Network requires a registration procedure for new users. The registration process is part of the shopping club's security system, designed to prevent unauthorized users from accessing the credit card information you supply to make purchases online.

Note

Efforts are underway to make credit-card orders over the Internet safe, but those efforts are incomplete. As things stand, your credit information can be stolen and misused. Exercise extreme caution when using a credit card online. It's safest to restrict your ordering to big operations such as ISN who have an interest in keeping your credit information secure to encourage confidence in their services.

■ **Deep Space Mall** (http://www.deepspace.com/deepspace.html)

An odd combination of shopping sites and links to space pictures. To each his own.

■ **One World Plaza** (http://www.digimark.net/windata)

Over 100 shops to browse. Bring lunch.

■ **Burlington Coat Factory** (http://www.coat.com)

Order anything from the bargain outlet clothing shop.

■ **Download Bookstore** (http://dab.psi.net/downloadbookstore)

An innovative online bookstore that lets you "try before you buy" by downloading excerpts or tables of contents from books before ordering.

■ **CDnow!** (http://cdnow.com)

An online CD store offering 140,000 recordings plus online copies of articles and reviews from music industry magazines.

Entertainment

■ **Top Ten Lists from *The Late Show with David Letterman*** (http://www.cbs.com/lateshow/ttlist.html)

The latest lists, plus archives of *all* the lists—even the ones that weren't funny.

■ **Cardiff Movie Database** (http://www.cm.cf.ac.uk/movies)

An elaborate database of *professional* film reviews ("Keanu Reeves can't talk"), film writing, graphics, and much more.

■ **Amateur Movie Reviews** (newsgroup rec.art.movies.reviews)

The opinions of your fellow movie fans plus the counterpoints of their colleagues. ("Keanu Reeves *can so* talk!")

■ **Buena Vista** (http://bvp.wdp.com)

Information, graphics, clips, and more about the Disney empire: Disney Pictures, Touchstone Pictures, and Hollywood Pictures.

■ **Fox Broadcasting** (http://www.eden.com/users/my-html/fox.html)

Everything about the rebel fourth network, including the latest about *The Simpsons* and *Melrose Place.* The site is not created and maintained by Fox but by *fans*—which can be for the better or worse, depending on how you look at it.

■ **Warner Brothers Records** (http://www.iuma.com/warner)

Complete information on the Warner's label, including tour dates of its artists, new CD releases, and even video clips of stars such as Madonna.

■ **The Rolling Stones** (http://www.stones.com)

Yes, the world's oldest working rock band has its own Web site to keep you informed about tour dates and to sell you licensed Stones merchandise.

■ **Ultimate TV List** (http://tvnet.com/TVnet.html)

A listing of links to much of the TV-related stuff all over the Net, including Web sites, Gophers, FTP files, and newsgroups. A great starting place for finding information about your favorite show.

Sports

■ **WWW/Sports** (http://tns-www.lcs.mit.edu/cgi-bin/sports)

Links and updates about sporting events all over the world.

■ **Sports Server** (http://www.nando.net/sptsserv.html)

Complete coverage of scores, stats, standings, and injuries for professional and college basketball, football, and baseball teams.

■ **Americas Cup** (http://www.ac95.org)

Everything about the world's biggest sailboat race and national pride surrogate, including photos, history, and more.

■ **Tour De France** (http://www.velonews.com/VeloNews)

Everything about the world's biggest bike race and national pride surrogate, including results, course maps, and more.

■ **Water Skiing** (http://www.primenet.com:80/~jodell)

Tournament schedules and results, pictures, and more about a sport I tried once and won't try again unless I become suicidally depressed.

Miscellaneous Weird and Interesting Stuff

■ **Vegetarian Pages** (http://catless.ncl.ac.uk/Vegetarian)

A great place to learn about veggie techniques, recipes, nutritional information, and events. Bring celery.

■ **Bookwire** (http://www.bookwire.com)

The first stop for information about books, Bookwire features *Publishers Weekly* bestseller lists, a title database, and hundreds of links to book-related resources elsewhere on the Internet.

■ **Westin Travel Guide** (http://www.westin.com)

An international travel guide with advisories, destination attractions, business and family travel planning, and, of course, Westin hotel reservations.

■ **The First Church of Cyberspace** (http://execpc.com/~chender)

Founded by a Presbyterian pastor in New Jersey, the First Church of Cyberspace features a sanctuary, a library, a gallery, a gathering place, and a multimedia bible. Other features include Sunday school classes and files of sermons from ministers across the country. Visitors are encouraged to practice "active worship" by responding to sermons and other material offered through the church. Obviously, the materials and activities are heavily Presbyterian—but everyone's welcome.

■ **Internal Revenue Service** (http://www.ustreas.gov/treasury/bureaus/irs/irs.html)

Yes, the IRS. You can get forms, look up rules, and communicate with the tax commissioner. (My dog ate the receipts. I swear.)

■ **Genealogy Home Page** (http://ftp.cac.psu.edu/~saw/genealogy.html)

Look up your family tree.

■ **The Wine Page** (http://augustus.csscr.washington.edu/personal/bigstar-mosaic/wine.html)

Everything about wine, including tasting notes and "virtual tasting" of online wine.

■ **Consumer Information Center** (http://www.gsa.gov/staff/pa/cic/cic.htm)

The U.S. government's incredible database of consumer information (see Figure 7.1), including guides to personal finance.

■ **Self-Help Psychology Magazine** (http://www.well.com/
user/selfhelp)

A Web page featuring helpful articles written by mental-
health experts for laypeople who have problems (or think
they have problems).

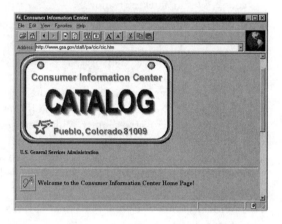

Figure 7.1. *The Consumer Information Center home page.*

By Laura Lemay

Your First Home Page

This chapter explains, briefly, how to create Web pages. The chapter gives you a brief overview of HTML, the language for writing WWW hypertext documents.

What HTML Is...and What It Isn't

There's one thing to note before you dive into actually writing Web pages: you should know what HTML is, what it can do, and what it can't do.

HTML stands for HyperText Markup Language. HTML is based on SGML (the Standard Generalized Markup Language), a much bigger document-processing system. SGML is used to describe the general structure of various kinds of documents. It is not a page description language like PostScript, nor is it a language that can be easily generated from your favorite page layout program. The primary focus of SGML, and therefore HTML, is the content of the document, not its appearance. This section explains a little bit more about that.

HTML Describes the Structure of a Document

HTML, by virtue of its SGML heritage, is a language for describing structured documents. The theory behind this is that most documents have common elements—titles, paragraphs, or lists—and if you define a set of elements that a document has before you start writing, you can label those parts of the document with the appropriate names. (See Figure 8.1.)

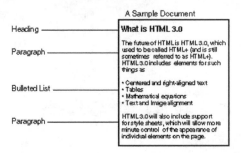

Figure 8.1. *Document elements.*

If you've worked with word processing programs that use style sheets (such as Microsoft Word) or paragraph catalogs (such as FrameMaker), then you've done something similar; each section of text conforms to one of a set of styles that are pre-defined before you start working.

The elements of a Web document are labeled through the use of HTML tags. It is the tags that describe the document; anything that it not a tag is part of the document itself.

What HTML Files Look Like

Documents written in HTML are in plain text (ASCII), and contain two things:

- The text of the document itself
- HTML tags that indicate document elements, structure, formatting, and hypertext links to other documents or to included media

Most HTML tags look something like this:

```
<TheTagName> affected text </TheTagName>
```

The tag name itself (here, `TheTagName`) is enclosed in brackets (`<>`).

HTML tags generally have a beginning and an ending tag, surrounding the text that they affect. The beginning tag "turns on" a feature (such as headings, bold, and so on), and the ending tag turns it off. Closing tags have the tag name preceded by a slash (`/`).

Not all HTML tags have a beginning and an end. Some tags are only one-sided, and still other tags are "containers" that hold extra information and text inside the brackets.

All HTML tags are case-insensitive; that is, you can specify them in upper- or lowercase, or in any mixture. So, `<HTML>` is the same as `<html>` is the same as `<HtMl>`. I like to put my tags in all caps (`<HTML>`) so I can pick them out from the text better. That's how I show them in the examples.

Exercise 1: Take a look at HTML sources.

Before you start writing your own HTML documents, it helps to get a feel for what an HTML document looks like. Luckily, there's plenty of unformatted source material out there for you to look at—every document that comes over the wire to your browser is in HTML format. (You usually only see the formatted version after the browser gets done with it.)

Most Web browsers have a way of letting you see the unformatted HTML source of a Web page. You may have a menu item or a button for View Source or View HTML. In Lynx, the \ (backslash) command toggles between source view and formatted view.

Some browsers do not have the capability to directly view the source of a Web document, but do allow you to save the current page as a file to your local disk. Under a dialog box for saving the file, there may be a menu of formats; for example, Text, PostScript, or HTML. You can save the current page as HTML and then open that file in a text editor or word processor to see the HTML source.

Try going to a typical home page, then viewing the source for that page. For example, Figure 8.2 shows what the normal NCSA Mosaic home page (`http://www.ncsa.uiuc.edu/SDG/Software/Mosaic/NCSAMosaicHome.html`) looks like.

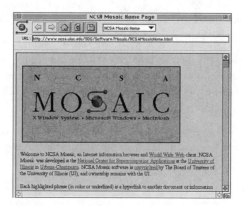

Figure 8.2. *Mosaic home page.*

The HTML source of that page should look something like Figure 8.3.

Figure 8.3. *Some HTML source.*

Try viewing the source of your own favorite Web pages. You should start seeing some similarities in the way pages are organized, and get a feel for the kinds of tags that HTML uses. You can learn a lot about HTML by comparing the text on the screen with the source for that text.

Exercise 2: Creating an HTML document.

To get started writing HTML, all you really need is something to edit your HTML files, and at least one browser to view them. You can create, link, and test whole suites of Web pages without even touching a network.

First, you'll need a text editor. A text editor is a program that saves files in ASCII format. That is, as just plain text, with no font formatting or special characters. On UNIX, the text editors are vi, emacs, or pico. On Windows, the built-in Notepad or DOS edit are good basic text editors, or a shareware editor such as WED or WinEdit will work as well. On the Macintosh, you can use the built-in SimpleText, or a more powerful text editor such as BBedit or Alpha (both of which are shareware).

If all you have is a word processor such as Microsoft Word, don't panic. Usually when you use the Save or Save As command there will be a menu of formats you can use to save the file. One of those should be "Text Only" or "Text Only with Line Breaks." Both of these options will save your file as plain ASCII, just as if you were using a text editor. For HTML files, you'll want to use the Text Only with Line Breaks option if you have it.

What about the plethora of editors that claim to help you write HTML easier? Most of them are actually simple text editors with some buttons that stick the tags in for you. If you've got one of those, go ahead and use it.

Open up that text editor, and type the following code:

```
<HTML><HEAD>
<TITLE>My Sample HTML Document</TITLE></HEAD>
<BODY>
<H1>This is an HTML Document</H1>
</BODY></HTML>
```

After you create your HTML file, save it to disk—and remember to save it as a text-only file if you're using a word processor. When you pick a name for the file, there are two rules to follow:

- The file name should have an extension of .html (.htm on DOS systems), for example, `myfile.html` or `text.html`.

- Use small, simple names. Avoid using spaces or special characters (bullets, accented characters and so on) in the filename, and be aware that upper- and lowercase are considered different in most Web software.

Now, start up your Web browser. You don't have to be connected to the network since you're not going to be opening documents at any other site. Your browser or network connection software may complain about the lack of a network connection, but usually it will eventually give up and let you use it anyway.

Once your browser is running, look for a menu item or button labeled Open Local, Open File, or sometimes just Open. It's a menu item that will let you browse your local disk. (In Lynx simply use the command `lynx myfile.html` from a command line.) The Open Local command (or its equivalent) tells the browser to read an HTML file from your disk, parse it, and display it, just as if it were a page already on the Web. Using your browser and the Open Local command, you can write and test your HTML files on your computer in the privacy of your own home.

Try opening up the little file you just created in your browser. You should see something like the picture shown in Figure 8.4.

If you don't see something like what's in the picture (for example, if parts are missing, or if everything looks like a heading), go back into your text editor and compare your file to the example. Make sure all your tags have closing tags, and that all your < characters are matched by > characters. You don't have to quit your browser to do this; just fix the file and save it again under the same name.

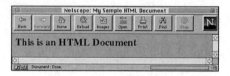

Figure 8.4. *The sample HTML file.*

Then go back to your browser. There should be a command called "Reload." (In Lynx, it's Control+R.) The browser will read the new version of your file, and voilà, you can edit and preview and edit and preview until you get it right.

A Note About Formatting

When an HTML document is parsed by a browser, any formatting you may have done by hand—that is, any extra spaces, tabs, returns, and so on—are ignored. The only thing that formats an HTML document is an HTML tag. If you spend hours carefully editing a plain text file to have nicely formatted paragraphs and columns of numbers, but do not include any tags, when you read the document into an HTML browser, all the text will flow all into one paragraph. All your work will have been in vain.

The advantage of having all white space (spaces, tabs, returns) ignored is that you can put your tags wherever you want.

Programs to Help You Write HTML

You may be thinking that all this tag stuff is a real pain, especially if you didn't get that small example right the first time. You have to remember all the tags. And you have to type them in right and close each one. What a hassle.

There are programs that can help you write HTML. These programs tend to fall into two categories: editors in which you write HTML directly, and converters, which convert the output of some other word processing program into HTML.

Editors

Many freeware and shareware programs are available for editing HTML files. Most of these programs are essentially text editors with extra menu items or buttons that insert the appropriate HTML tags into your text. HTML-based text editors are particularly nice for two reasons: You don't have to remember all the tags, and you don't have to take the time to type them all.

For now, if you have an HTML editor, feel free to use it for the examples in this book. If all you have is a text editor, no problem; it just means you'll have to do a little more typing.

What about WYSIWYG editors? The problem is that there's really no such thing as WYSIWYG when you're dealing with HTML, since WYG can vary wildly based on the browser that someone is using to read your document. So you could spend hours in a so-called WYSIWYG HTML editor, only to discover that when the HTML output of that editor is read on some other browser, it looks truly awful. So although there are semi-WYSIWYG editors for HTML, keep in mind HTML's design and limitations when you use them.

Converters

In addition to the HTML editors, there are also converters, which take files from many popular word-processing programs and convert them to HTML. This is the closest HTML gets to being

WYSIWYG. With a simple set of templates, you can write your documents entirely in your favorite program. Then, convert the result. You'll almost never have to deal with all this non-WYSIWYG text-only tag nonsense.

In many cases, converters can be extremely useful, particularly for putting existing documents on the Web as fast as possible. However, converters are in no way an ideal environment for HTML development. Most converter programs are fairly limited, not necessarily by their own features, but mostly by the limitations in HTML itself. No amount of fancy converting is going to make HTML do things that it can't yet do. If a particular capability doesn't exist in HTML, there's nothing the converter can do to solve that (and it may end up doing strange things to your HTML files, causing you more work than if you just did all the formatting yourself).

The other problem with converters is that, even though you can do most of your writing and development in a converter with a simple set of formats and low expectations, you will usually have to go "under the hood" and edit the HTML text yourself. Most converters do not convert images, or automate links to documents out on the Web.

In other words, even if you've already decided that you want to do the bulk of your Web work using a converter, you'll still need to know HTML. So press onward; there's not that much to learn.

Structuring Your HTML

HTML defines three tags that are used to describe the document's overall structure and provide some simple "header" information. These three tags identify your document to browsers or HTML tools. They also provide simple information about the document (such as its title or who wrote it) before loading the entire thing. The document structure tags don't affect what the document looks like when it's displayed; they're only there to help tools that interpret or filter HTML files.

According to the strict HTML definition, these tags are optional. If your document does not contain them, browsers will be able to read it anyway. However, it is possible that these document structure tags might become required elements in the future. It's also possible that tools may come along that need them. If you get into the habit of including the document structure tags now, you won't have to worry about updating all your files later.

<HTML>

The first document structure tag in every HTML document is the <HTML> tag. It indicates that the content of this file is in the HTML language.

All the text and HTML commands in your HTML document should go within the beginning and ending HTML tags, like this:

```
<HTML>
...your document...
</HTML>
<HEAD>
```

The <HEAD> tag specifies that the lines within the beginning and ending points of the tag are the prologue to the rest of the file. There are generally only a few tags that go into the <HEAD> portion of the document (most notably, the document title, described below). You should never put any of the text of your document into the header.

Here's a typical example of how you would properly use the <HEAD> tag (you'll learn about </TITLE> later):

```
<HTML>
<HEAD>
<TITLE>This is the Title.</TITLE>
</HEAD>
....
</HTML>
<BODY>
```

The remainder of your HTML document, including all the text and other content (links, pictures, and so on) is enclosed within a <BODY> tag. In combination with the <HTML> and <HEAD> tags, this looks like:

```
<HTML>
<HEAD>
<TITLE>This is the Title. It will be explained later on</TITLE>
</HEAD>
<BODY>
....
</BODY>
</HTML>
```

The Title

Each HTML document needs a title to indicate what the document describes. The title is used by your browser's bookmarks or hotlist program, and also by other programs that catalogue Web pages. To give a document a title, use the <TITLE> tag. <TITLE> tags always go inside the document header (the <HEAD> tags), and describe the contents of the page, like this:

```
<HTML>
<HEAD>
<TITLE>The Lion, The Witch, and the Wardrobe</TITLE>
</HEAD>
<BODY>
....
</BODY>
</HTML>
```

You can only have one title in the document, and that title can only contain plain text; that is, there shouldn't be any other tags inside the title.

When you pick a title, try to pick one that is both short and descriptive of the content on the page. Additionally, your title should also be relevant out of context. If someone browsing on the Web followed a random link and ended up on this page, or if they found your title in a friend's browser history list, would they have any idea what this page is about? You may not intend the page to be used independently of the documents you specifically linked to it, but because anyone can link to any page at any time, be prepared for that consequence and pick a helpful title.

Additionally, because many browsers put the title in the title bar of the window, you may have a limited number of words available. (Although the text within the <TITLE> tag can be of any length, it may be cut off by the browser when it's displayed.) Here are some other examples of good titles:

```
<TITLE>Poisonous Plants of North America</TITLE>
<TITLE>Image Editing: A Tutorial</TITLE>
<TITLE>Upcoming Cemetery Tours, Summer 1995</TITLE>
<TITLE>Installing The Software: Opening the CD Case</TITLE>
<TITLE>Laura Lemay's Awesome Home Page</TITLE>
```

And some not-so-good titles:

```
<TITLE>Part Two</TITLE>
<TITLE>An Example</TITLE>
<TITLE>Nigel Franklin Hobbes</TITLE>
<TITLE>Minutes of the Second Meeting of the Fourth
Conference of the Committee for the Preservation of
English Roses, Day Four, After Lunch</TITLE>
```

The following examples show how titles look in both Netscape (Figure 8.5) and Lynx (Figure 8.6).

```
<TITLE>Poisonous Plants of North America</TITLE>
```

Figure 8.5. *The output in Netscape.*

```
Poisonous Plants of North America
```

Figure 8.6. *The output in Lynx.*

Headings

Headings are used to divide sections of text, just like this book is divided. ("Headings," above, is a heading.) HTML defines six levels of headings. Heading tags look like this:

```
<H1>Installing Your Safetee Lock</H1>
```

The numbers indicate heading levels (H1 through H6). The headings, when they're displayed, are not numbered. They are displayed either in bigger or bolder text, or are centered or underlined, or are capitalized—something that makes them stand out from regular text.

Think of the headings as items in an outline. If the text you're writing has a structure, use the headings to indicate that structure, as shown in the next code lines. (Note that I've indented the headings in this example to show the hierarchy better. They don't have to be indented in your document, and, in fact, the indenting will be ignored by the browser.)

```
<H1>Engine Tune-Up</H1>
    <H2>Change The Oil</H2>
    <H2>Adjust the Valves</H2>
    <H2>Change the Spark Plugs</H2>
        <H3>Remove the Old Plugs</H3>
        <H3>Prepare the New Plugs</H3>
            <H4>Remove the Guards</H4>
            <H4>Check the Gap</H4>
            <H4>Apply Anti-Seize Lubricant</H4>
            <H4>Install the Plugs</H4>
    <H2>Adjust the Timing</H2>
```

Note that (unlike titles), headings can be any length, including lines and lines of text (although because headings are emphasized, having lines and lines of emphasized text may be tiring for your reader).

It's a common practice to use a first-level heading at the top of your document to either duplicate the title (which is usually displayed elsewhere), or to provide a shorter or less contextual form of the title. For example, if you had a page that showed several examples of folding bedsheets, part of a long document on how to fold bedsheets, the title might look something like this:

```
<TITLE>How to Fold Sheets: Some Examples</TITLE>
```

The top-most heading, however, might just say:

```
<H1>Examples</H1>
```

Don't use headings to display text in boldface type, or to make certain parts of your document stand out more. Although it may look cool on your browser, you don't know what it'll look like when other people use their browsers to read your document. Other browsers may number headings, or format them in a manner that you don't expect. Also, tools to create searchable indexes of Web pages may extract your headings to indicate the important parts of a document. By using headings for something other than an actual heading, you may be foiling those search programs and creating strange results.

The following examples show headings and how they appear in Netscape (Figure 8.7) and Lynx (Figure 8.8):

```
<H1>Engine Tune-Up</H1>
    <H2>Change The Oil</H2>
    <H2>Change the Spark Plugs</H2>
        <H3>Prepare the New Plugs</H3>
            <H4>Remove the Guards</H4>
            <H4>Check the Gap</H4>
```

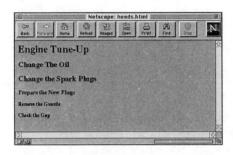

Figure 8.7. *The output in Netscape.*

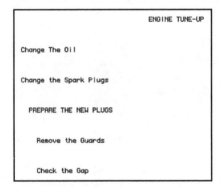

Figure 8.8. *The output in Lynx.*

Paragraphs

Now that you have a document title and several headings, let's add some ordinary paragraphs to the document.

Unfortunately, paragraphs in HTML are slippery things. Between the three versions of HTML, the definition of a paragraph has changed. The only thing the three versions agree on is that you indicate a plain text paragraph using the <P> tag.

The first version of HTML specified the <P> tag as a one-sided tag. There was no corresponding </P>, and the <P> tag was used to indicate the end of a paragraph (a paragraph break), not the beginning. So paragraphs in the first version of HTML looked like this:

```
The blue sweater was reluctant to be worn, and wrestled
with her as she attempted to put it on. The collar was
too small, and would not fit over her head, and the arm
holes moved seemingly randomly away from her searching
hands.<P>
Exasperated, she took off the sweater and flung it on the
floor. Then she vindictively stomped on it in revenge for
its recalcitrant behavior.<P>
```

Most browsers that were created early on in the history of the Web—and many browsers still—assume that paragraphs will be formatted this way. When they come across a <P> tag, they start a new line and add some extra vertical space between the line they just ended and the one that they just began, as shown in Figure 8.9.

Space between paragraphs

Figure 8.9. *How paragraphs are formatted.*

In the HTML 2.0 and the proposed HTML 3.0 specifications, the paragraph tag has been revised. In these versions of HTML, the paragraph tags are two-sided (<P>...</P>), but <P> indicates the beginning of the paragraph. Also, the closing tag (</P>) is optional. So the sweater story would look like this in the newer versions of HTML:

```
<P>The blue sweater was reluctant to be worn, and
wrestled with her as she attempted to put it on. The
collar was too small, and would not fit over her head,
and the arm holes moved seemingly randomly away from her
searching hands.
</P><P>Exasperated, she took of the sweater and flung it
on the floor. Then she vindictively stomped on it in
revenge for its recalcitrant behavior.</P>
```

It's a good idea to get into the habit of using <P> at the start of a paragraph, as this will become important in HTML 3.0, where you can define the alignment and other features of each paragraph. Older browsers will accept this form of paragraphs just fine.

However, note that because many browsers still expect <P> to indicate the end of a paragraph, if you use it at the beginning you may end up with extra space in between the first paragraph and the element before it.

If this bothers you overly much, you can do one of the following:

- Go back to the old style of defining paragraphs.
- Use <P> as a paragraph separator, rather than indicating the beginning or ending of a paragraph.
- Leave off the first <P> in each set of paragraphs.

Some people like to use <P> tags to spread out the text on the page. Once again, the cardinal reminder: Design for content, not for appearance. Someone with a text-based browser is not going to care much about the extra space you so carefully put in, and some browsers may even collapse multiple <P> tags into one, erasing all your careful formatting.

The following example shows a sample paragraph and how it appears in Netscape (Figure 8.10) and Lynx (Figure 8.11).

```
<P>The sweater lay quietly on the floor, seething from
its ill treatment. It wasn't its fault that it didn't fit
right. It hadn't wanted to be purchased by this ill-
mannered woman.</P>
```

Figure 8.10. *The output in Netscape.*

```
The sweater lay quietly on the floor, seething from its ill treatment.
It wasn't its fault that it didn't fit right. It hadn't wanted to be
purchased by this ill-mannered woman.
```

Figure 8.11. *The output in Lynx.*

Comments

You can put comments into HTML documents to describe the document itself or to provide some kind of indication of the status of the document; some source code control programs can put document status into comments, for example. Text in comments is ignored when the HTML file is parsed; comments don't ever show up on screen—that's why they're comments. Comments look like this:

```
<!— This is a comment —>
```

Each line should be individually commented, and it's usually a good idea not to include other HTML tags within comments. (Although this practice isn't strictly illegal, many browsers may get confused when they encounter HTML tags within comments and display them anyway.)

Here are some examples:

```
<!— Rewrite this section with less humor —>
<!— Neil helped with this section —>
<!— Go Tigers! —>
```

Exercise 3: Creating a real HTML document.

At this point, you should know enough to get started creating simple HTML documents. You understand what HTML is, you've been introduced to a handful of tags, and you've even tried browsing an HTML file. You haven't done any links yet, but you'll get to that soon enough.

This exercise shows you how to create an HTML file that uses the tags you've learned about in this chapter. It will give you a feel for what the tags look like when they're displayed on-screen and for the sorts of typical mistakes you're going to make.

So, create a simple example in that text editor of yours. It doesn't have to say much of anything; in fact, all it needs to include are the structure tags, a title, a couple of headings, and a paragraph or two. Here's an example:

```
<HTML>
<HEAD>
<TITLE>Company Profile, Camembert Incorporated</TITLE>
</HEAD>
<BODY>
<H1>Camembert Incorporated</H1>
"Many's the long night I dreamed of cheese — toasted,
mostly." — Robert Louis Stevenson
<H2>What We Do</H2>
We make cheese. Lots of cheese; more than eight tons of
cheese a year. Your Brie, your Gouda, your Havarti, we
make it all.
<H2>Why We Do It</H2>
<P>We are paid an awful lot of money by people who like
cheese. So we make more.</P>
</BODY>
</HTML>
```

Save your example to an HTML file, open it in your browser, and see how it came out.

If you have access to another browser on your platform, or on another platform, I highly recommend opening the same HTML file there so you can see the differences in appearance between browsers. Sometimes the differences can surprise you; lines that looked fine in one browser will look strange in another browser.

For example, the cheese factory example looks like Figure 8.13 in Netscape (the Macintosh version) and like Figure 8.14 in Lynx.

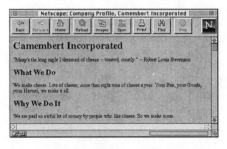

Figure 8.12. *The cheese factory in Netscape.*

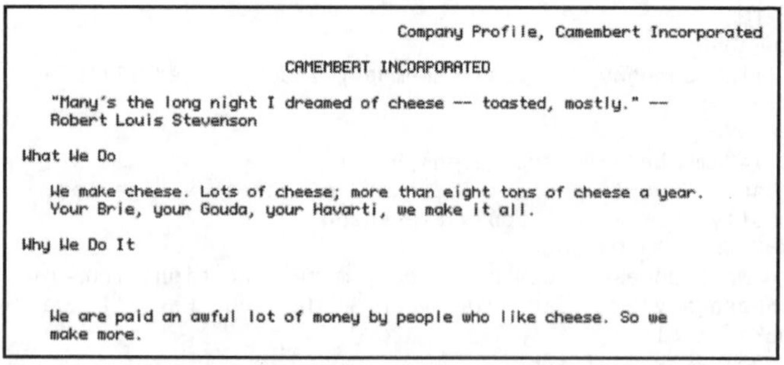

```
                                    Company Profile, Camembert Incorporated
                         CAMEMBERT INCORPORATED

    "Many's the long night I dreamed of cheese -- toasted, mostly." --
    Robert Louis Stevenson

  What We Do

      We make cheese. Lots of cheese; more than eight tons of cheese a year.
      Your Brie, your Gouda, your Havarti, we make it all.

  Why We Do It


      We are paid an awful lot of money by people who like cheese. So we
      make more.
```

Figure 8.13. *The cheese factory in Lynx.*

The next section explains links, but before we move on, here's a quick-reference table of the HTML tags you've learned so far:

Table 8.1. HTML tags.

Tag	Use
<HTML> ... </HTML>	The entire HTML document
<HEAD> ... </HEAD>	The head, or prologue, of the HTML document
<BODY> ... </BODY>	All the other content in the HTML document
<TITLE> ... </TITLE>	The title of the document
<H1> ... </H1>	First-level heading
<H2> ... </H2>	Second-level heading
<H3> ... </H3>	Third-level heading
<H4> ... </H4>	Fourth-level heading
<H5> ... </H5>	Fifth-level heading
<H6> ... </H6>	Sixth-level heading
<P> ... </P>	Paragraph
<! — ... —>	Comment

Putting the Hyper in Hypertext: All About Links

You now have two documents that have some headings and text in them. This is all well and good, but rather boring. The real fun

starts when you learn how to do hypertext links and link up all
your documents to the Web. This section starts you going on
creating links.

Creating Links

To create a link in HTML, you need two things:

- The name of the file (or the URL of the file) you want to
  link to
- The text that will serve as the "hot spot"—that is, the text
  that will be highlighted in the browser, which your readers
  can then select to follow the link

Only the second element is actually visible in your document.
When your reader selects the text that points to a link, the browser
uses the first element to "jump" to the appropriate document.
That is, the browser uses the first element to retrieve the linked
document from the disk or from over the Net, to parse the
HTML that document contains (if necessary), and to display it.

The Link Tag <A>

To create a link in an HTML document, you use the HTML link
tag <A>...</A>. The <A> tag is often called an anchor tag, as it can
also be used to create anchors for links. The most common use of
the link tag, however, is to create links to other documents.

Unlike the simple tags, the <A> tag has some extra features: the
opening tag, <A>, includes both the name of the tag ("A"), and
extra information about the link itself. The extra features are called
attributes of the tag. So instead of the opening tag just having a
name inside brackets, it looks something like this:

```
<A NAME="Up" HREF="../menu.html" TITLE="Ostrich Care">
```

The extra attributes (in this example, NAME, HREF, and TITLE)
describe the link itself. Many of the attributes are only useful for
special HTML tools and browsers that can do fancy things with
the links. The attribute you'll probably use the most often is the
HREF attribute, short for "Hypertext REFerence." The HREF

attribute is used to specify the name or URL of the file where this link points.

Like most HTML tags, the link tag also has a closing tag, `</A>`. All of the text between the opening and closing tags will become the actual link on the screen and be highlighted or underlined or blue or red when the Web page is displayed. That's the text you or your reader will click on (or select, in browsers that don't use mice) to jump to the document specified by the HREF attribute.

Figure 8.14 shows the parts of a typical link using the `<A>` tag, including the HREF, the text of the link, and the closing tag:

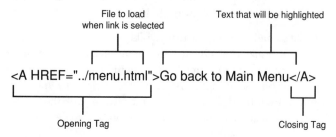

Figure 8.14. *An HTML link using the `<A>` tag.*

The following two examples show a simple link and what it looks like in Netscape (Figure 8.15) and Lynx (Figure 8.16).

```
Go back to <A HREF="../menu.html">Main Menu</A>
```

Figure 8.15. *The output in Netscape.*

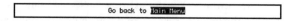

Figure 8.16. *The output in Lynx.*

Exercise 4: Link two documents.

Let's try a really simple example, with two HTML documents on your local disk. You'll need your text editor and a Web browser for this, but since both the documents you'll be fooling with are on your local disk, you won't need to be connected to the network.

First, create two HTML documents, and save them in separate files. Here's the code for the two HTML files I created for this section, which I called menu.html and feeding.html. It really doesn't matter what your two documents look like or what they're called, but make sure you put in your own file names if you're following along with this example.

The first file is called menu.html file, and it looks like this:

```
<HTML>
<HEAD>
<TITLE>How To Care For Your Ostrich</TITLE>
</HEAD><BODY>
<H1>Caring for Your New Ostrich</H1>
<P>Your new ostrich is a delicate and sensitive creature.
This document describes how to care for your ostrich so
that he can be a happy and healthy ostrich and give you
hours of fun and friendship.</P>
<P>Feeding Your Ostrich</P>
<P>Grooming Your Ostrich</P>
<P>Cleaning Up After Your Ostrich</P>
<P>Taunting Your Ostrich</P>
</BODY>
</HTML>
```

The list of menu items ("Feeding Your Ostrich," "Grooming Your Ostrich," and so on) will be links to other documents. For now, just type them as regular text; you'll turn them into links later.

The second file, feeding.html, looks like this:

```
<HTML>
<HEAD>
<TITLE>How To Care For Your Ostrich: Feeding Your
Ostrich</TITLE>
</HEAD><BODY>
```

```
<H1>Feeding Your Ostrich</H1>
<P>This section describes what, how often, and how to
feed your ostrich
</P>
<H2>What to Feed Your Ostrich</H2>
Ostriches benefit best from a balanced diet such as that
provided by United Bird Food's Ostrich Kibble 102. We
recommend feeding your ostrich a cup of kibbles once a
day, with ample water.
<H2>How to Feed Your Ostrich</H2>
<P>To feed your ostrich, leave the ostrich kibbles in a
container by the edge of the ostrich's pen.</P>
<P>NOTE: Ostriches do not like being watched while
eating, and may attack you if you stand too close. We
recommend leaving your ostrich to eat in peace.
</P>
<P>Go back to Main Menu</P>
</BODY>
</HTML>
```

Make sure both your files are in the same directory or folder, and
if you haven't called them menu.html and feeding.html, make
sure that you take note of the names because you'll need them
later.

First, create a link from the menu file to the feeding file. Edit the
menu.html file, and put the cursor at the line that says <P>Feeding
Your Ostrich</P>.

Link tags do not define the format of the text itself, so leave in the
paragraph tags and just add the link inside the paragraph. First,
put in the link tags themselves (the <A> and </A> tags) around the
text that you want to use as the link:

<P><A>Feeding Your Ostrich</A></P>

Now add the name of the file you want to link to as the HREF part
of the opening link tag. Enclose the name of the file in quotes,
with an equals sign between HREF and the name. Note that upper
and lower case are distinct, so make sure you type the file name
exactly as it appears on the disk. Here I've used feeding.html; if
you used different files, use a different file name.

<P><A HREF="feeding.html">Feeding Your Ostrich</A></P>

Now, start up your browser, select Open Local (or its equivalent), and open the menu.html file. The paragraph that you used as your link should now show up as a link that is in a different color, underlined, or otherwise highlighted. Figure 8.17 shows how it looked when I opened it in the Macintosh version of Netscape:

And now, when you click on the link, your browser should load in and display the feeding.html document, as shown in Figure 8.18.

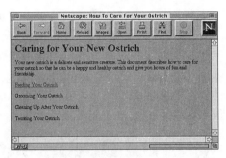

Figure 8.17. *The* menu.html *file with link.*

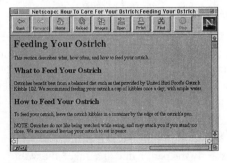

Figure 8.18. *The* feeding.html *document.*

If your browser can't find the file when you choose the link, make sure that the name of the file in the HREF part of the link tag is the same as the name of the file on the disk and that both of the files are in the same directory. Remember to close your link, using the </A> tag, at the end of the text that serves as the link. Also, make sure that you have quotes at the end of the file name (sometimes it's easy to forget). All of these things can confuse the browser so that it cannot find the file or display the link properly.

Now, let's create a link from the feeding document back to the menu. There is a paragraph at the end of the `feeding.html` document intended for just this purpose:

```
<P>Go back to Main Menu</P>
```

Add the link tag with the appropriate HREF to that line, like this, where `menu.html` is the original menu file:

```
<P><A HREF="menu.html">Go back to Main Menu</A></P>
```

Now when you reload the "feeding" file, the link will be active, and you can jump between the menu and the feeding file by selecting those links.

Linking Local Documents Using Relative and Absolute Path Names

The example in the previous section shows how to link together documents that are contained in the same folder on your local disk (called, appropriately, local documents). This section continues that thread, linking documents that are still on the local disk, but may be contained in different directories on that disk.

Relative Path Names

When you specify the path name of a linked file within quotes, as you did earlier, the browser looks for it in the same directory as the current file. This is so, even if that browser is looking at that file over the Net from some faraway place. This is the simplest form of a relative path name.

Relative path names can also include directories, or they can point to the path you would take to navigate to that file if you started at the current directory or folder. A path name might include directions, for example, to go up two directory levels, and then go down two other directories to get to the file.

To specify relative path names in links, use UNIX-style path names, regardless of the system you actually have. This means that directory or folder names are separated by forward slashes (/), and you use two dots to refer to the directory above the current one (..).

Table 8.2 shows some examples of relative path names and what they mean.

Table 8.2. Relative path names.

Path name	Means
HREF="file.html"	file.html is located in the current directory.
HREF="files/file.html"	file.html is located in the directory (or folder) called files (and the files directory is located in the current directory).
HREF="files/morefiles/file.html"	file.html is located in the morefiles directory, which is located in the files directory, which is located in the current directory.
HREF="../file.html"	file.html is located in the directory (or folder) one level up from the current directory.
HREF="../../files/file.html"	file.html is located two directory levels up, in the directory files.

If you're linking files on a personal computer (Mac or PC) and you want to link to a file on a different disk, use the name or letter of the disk as just another directory name in the relative path.

On the Macintosh, the name of the disk is used just as it appears on the disk itself. Assume you have a disk called Hard Disk 2, and your HTML files are contained in a folder called HTML Files. If you wanted to link to a file called jane.html in a folder called Public on a shared disk called Jane's Mac, you could use the following relative path name:

```
HREF="../../Jane's Mac/Public/jane.html"
```

On DOS systems, the disks are referred to by letter, just as you would expect them to be, but instead of being c:, d:, and so on, substitute a vertical bar (¦) for the colon (the colon has a special meaning in link path names), and don't forget to use forward slashes like on UNIX. So, if the current file is located in C:\FILES\HTML\, and you want to link to D:\FILES.NEW\ HTML\MORE\INDEX.HTM, the relative path name to that file would be:

```
HREF="../../d¦/files.new/html/more/index.htm"
```

Absolute Path Names

You can also specify the link to another document on your local system using an absolute path name. Relative path names, as described above, point to the document you want to link by describing its relation to the current document. Absolute path names, on the other hand, point to the document by starting at the top level of your directory hierarchy and working downward through all the intervening directories to reach the file.

Absolute path names always begin with a slash, which is the way they are differentiated from relative path names. Following the slash are all directories in the path from the top level to the file you are linking.

Table 8.3 shows some examples of absolute path names and what they mean.

Table 8.3. Absolute path names.

Path name	Means
HREF="/u1/lemay/file.html"	file.html is located in the directory /u1/lemay.
HREF="/d¦/files/html/file.htm"	file.htm is located on the D: disk in the directories files/html (DOS systems).
HREF="/Hard Disk 1/ Files/file.html"	file.html is HTML located on the disk Hard Disk 1, in the folder HTML Files (typically a Macintosh).

Should You Use Relative or Absolute Path Names?

To link your own documents, 99 percent of the time you should use relative path names instead of the absolute path names. Using absolute path names may seem easier for complicated links between lots of documents, but absolute path names are not portable. If you specify your links as absolute path names and you move your files elsewhere on the disk, or rename a directory or a disk listed in that absolute path, then all your links will break and you'll have to laboriously edit all your HTML files and fix them all. Using absolute path names also makes it very difficult to move your files to a Web server when you decide to actually make them available on the Web—and that's what you're reading this book for, isn't it?

Specifying relative path names allows you to move your documents around on your own system and to move them to other systems with little to no file modifications to fix the links. It's much easier to maintain HTML documents with relative path names, so the extra work of setting them initially is often well worth the effort.

Links to Other Documents on the Web

So now you have a whole set of documents, all linked to each other. In some places in your documents, however, you would like to refer to a page somewhere else on the Net; for example, to the Palo Alto Zoo home page for more information on the socialization of ostriches. You can also use the link tag to link those other documents on the Net, which I'll call remote documents.

The HTML code you use to link documents on the Web looks exactly the same as the code you used for links between local documents. You still use the <A> tag with an HREF attribute, and include some text to serve as the link on your Web page. But instead of a file name or a path in the HREF, use the URL of that document on the Web, as Figure 8.19 shows.

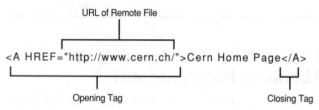

Figure 8.19. *Link to remote files.*

Exercise 8.5: Linking your ostrich pages to the Web.

Let's go back to those two documents you linked together earlier in this chapter, the ones about ostriches. The menu.html file contained several links to other local documents that described how to take care of your ostrich.

Now let's say you want to add a link to the bottom of the menu file to point to the ostrich archives at the Palo Alto Zoo (the world's leading authority on the care of ostriches), whose URL is http://www.zoo.palo-alto.ca.us/ostriches/home.html.

> **Note:** I'm making most of this up. Although the city of Palo Alto, California, has a Web page (`http://www.city.palo-alto.ca.us/home.html`), Palo Alto doesn't have a zoo with ostriches (they do have a petting zoo, however). For the purposes of this example, just pretend that there's a Web page for the Palo Alto Zoo.

First, add the appropriate text for the link to your menu page:

```
<P>The Palo Alto Zoo has more information on ostriches</P>
```

What if you don't know the URL of the home page for the Palo Alto Zoo (or the document you want to link to), but you do know how to get to it by following several links on several different people's home pages? Not a problem. Use your browser to find the home page for the document you want to link to. (Figure 8.20 shows what the home page for the Palo Alto Zoo might look like, if it existed.)

Most browsers display the URL of the file they're currently looking at in a box somewhere near the top of the page. This makes it particularly easy for you to link to other documents; all you have to do is go there with your browser, copy the URL from the window, and paste it into the HTML page you're working on. No typing!

Figure 8.20. *The Palo Alto Zoo home page.*

Once you have the URL of the zoo (the URL for that page is in the box in the top corner, and you can usually copy from that box), you can construct a link tag in your menu file and paste the appropriate URL into the link:

```
<P>The <A HREF="http://www.zoo.palo-alto.ca.us/ostriches/
home.html">Palo Alto Zoo</A>
has more information on ostriches</P>
```

Of course, if you already know the URL of the page you want to link to, you can just type it into the HREF part of the link. Keep in mind, however, that if you make a mistake your browser won't be able to find the file on the other end. Most URLs are a little too complex for normal humans to be able to remember them; I prefer to copy and paste whenever I can to cut down on the chances of typing them wrong.

Figure 8.21 shows how the menu.html file, with the new link in it, looks when it is displayed by Netscape.

Figure 8.21. *The Palo Alto Zoo link.*

By Laura Lemay

Future Developments in HTML and the Web

HTML 3.0 is on the cutting edge. It's the next big thing as far as the HTML language itself is concerned. But what about the very bleeding edge? What's after HTML 3.0? What other interesting things are going on with the Web that might become more important or change how we use and develop pages for the Web in the future? In this chapter, I'll cover some of the more interesting proposals and techniques that are emerging. Some of these are things you can play with now; some of them are in the distant future. All of them are interesting in the possibilities they have for changing the face of the Web.

Style Sheets

Style sheets provide a method for defining how a particular HTML tag will appear on the screen, such as its font, font size, color, or the space around it. Style sheets provide better control over presentations, which so many Web authors have wanted, while allowing HTML to remain primarily a simple and small content-based language.

One important thing to note, however, is that style sheets provide presentation *hints* for the browser to interpret—not absolute commandments for how the document should look. If the browser does not have the font or other capabilities that you've specified in your style sheet, the browser can substitute as necessary. Or, the user might also decide to override your carefully tuned defaults. So, if you're looking for monomaniacal control over your presentation, style sheets won't make you happy (and perhaps you should move on to the next section on Acrobat and PDF files). But style sheets do go a significant distance toward making HTML genuinely pleasant to use.

The current HTML 3.0 specification provides a mechanism for allowing style sheets to be attached to HTML documents (through the <LINK> and <STYLE> tags) and provides a mechanism for creating differently styled paragraphs and other text elements that style sheets can hook onto (using CLASS). But it does not define what the style sheet language is and how it should be used. That will have to wait until HTML 3.1.

Currently, several style sheet proposals are on the table for HTML. The two most prominent are DSSSL-Lite, the style sheet of choice for the SGML Open Consortium, and CSS (Cascading Style Sheets), which was defined and developed by Håkon Lie at the World Wide Web Consortium. An experimental version of the latter is being implemented in Arena, the W3's HTML 3 browser, and in William Perry's emacs-w3 as well.

DSSSL-Lite

DSSSL stands for Document Style Semantics and Specification Language (whew!), which is a general proposal for creating style sheets for SGML documents and is fast on its way to becoming an ISO standard (or, as fast as the ISO organizations move, which isn't very fast). DSSSL has two main parts: a transformation process that organizes an SGML-conforming document into another SGML document (often a simpler one for the purposes of formatting, because you might have multiple content-based tags that apply to the same style characteristics), and a formatting process that applies hierarchical styles to the various parts of the SGML document.

Note

Of course, this is a gross oversimplification. Given that the DSSSL specification is 150 pages long and quite dense, explaining DSSSL correctly in less than several pages becomes difficult. This chapter gives you simply an overview of DSSSL.

DSSSL-Lite is a subset of DSSSL that provides a first step for SGML developers who want to eventually develop the full DSSSL but have to wait until the standard is settled. DSSSL-Lite contains only the formatting part of DSSSL and is limited to specific kinds of documents, particularly online documents without strict page boundaries that are read left to right (such as HTML documents).

DSSSL style sheets are written in a language based on Scheme, which is in turn a dialect of Lisp. DSSSL-Lite style sheets look something like the following (which is taken directly from the HTML style sheet by James Clark):

```
(element h1
    (paragraph
    font-size: very-large-font-size
    font-weight: 'bold
    display-alignment: 'center
    space-before: big-space-before
    space-after: big-space-after
    content: (sequence
        (literal
        (format-number (child-number) "1"))
        (literal ". ")
        (process-children))))
```

This example defines the style for an H1 tag, which would be a very large bold font (very-large-font-size was defined elsewhere in the style sheet as 36 point) that is centered, with lots of space before and after (defined elsewhere as 24 points), and numbered.

Cascading Style Sheets (CSS)

Cascading style sheets, or CSS, is a proposal by Håkon Lie of the W3 for creating hierarchies of style sheets that can be defined on several levels (such as site-wide, group-wide, or in individual pages) and can be overridden by the user in the browser. CSS is less concerned with the actual mechanics of what the style sheet language looks like and what it can do than it is with providing a simple and easy-to-understand structure in which presentation hints can be added to HTML documents and changed on multiple levels.

CSS style sheets, like all style sheets, are defined in an HTML document through the use of <LINK> and <STYLE>. The <LINK> tag points to externally defined style sheets, perhaps several of them, each one further defining and merging with the style in the previous style sheet. The <STYLE> tag defines further specifications for the current page, and its definitions are also merged into the overall style definitions. Finally, the user can also define style properties on the browser side that define things still further. (Remember, style sheets provide presentation hints, not absolute commandments.)

CSS provides a simple method of defining style properties that draws influence from X11 properties. Individual lines define a particular style characteristic, with the tag (or tag and class) they affect, the property to change, and the new value. A sample style sheet might look something like this (which is from Arena):

```
h1: align = left
h1: color.text = #900000
h1: margin.top = 10
h2: align = left
h2: color.text = #900000
h3: align = left
h3: margin.left = 0
h3: color.text = #900000

ul: indent = 20
ul: margin.left = 30
ul: margin.top = 4
ul: margin.bottom = 4
ul: color.text = #000000
dl: margin.left = 30p:
margin.left = 30

p: color.text = #000000
address: color.text = #008000
address: align = left
address: margin.left = 30
address: margin.right = 30

em: color.text = #00B000
a: color.text = #0050C0
```

```
h4: margin.left = 0
h5: margin.left = 0
h6: margin.left = 0
```

Which One?

Which style sheet standard will be the right one to use? Which one will be recommended by HTML 3.0? It's still far too early to tell.

CSS has the advantage over DSSSL-Lite right now in the Web community because browsers are beginning to support it and it's simple and easy to write. (You don't have to know Lisp to do it.) On the other hand, DSSSL-Lite is more general and powerful and has lots of support in the SGML standards community. Which style sheet proposal becomes "standard"—DSSSL-Lite, CSS, or some other proposal—is yet to be determined. Until HTML 3.0 becomes more widely supported, style sheets probably will not gain enough momentum for the decision to be made. But, considering how quickly things move in the Web industry, that might be sooner than we think.

Where to Get More Information

The best source of information about style sheets and the various style sheet proposals is on the W3's style sheet page at `http://www.w3.org/hypertext/WWW/Style/`. The pages linked to from there include Jim Clark's DSSSL page (`http://www.jclark.com/dsssl/`), the draft CSS proposal (`http://www.w3.org/hypertext/WWW/Style/css/draft.html`), and pointers to Arena and emacs-W3, as well as extensive background information on the issues that style sheets are intending to solve and how to go about solving them.

Adobe Acrobat (PDF) Files

If your documents rely heavily on complex page layout, you might want to consider distributing them as Adobe Acrobat files, because Acrobat retains all the original layout in your document. If your ears perked up at that, read on.

Adobe Acrobat files are created by the Adobe Acrobat program and are stored in a file format called PDF. PDF stands for

Portable Document Format; it's a way to represent a document with all its layout and fonts intact on multiple platforms. PDF documents are not HTML. They are an independent format, written by Adobe.

To read PDF files, you need the Adobe Acrobat reader. Figure 9.1 shows an example of the Acrobat reader on the Macintosh, with a sample PDF file being viewed. You can get the reader as an external application from Adobe's home page (http://www.adobe.com) and set it up as a helper application in your browser. Then, when you download PDF documents from Web pages, the reader will be launched, and you can read the documents from there. The reader is available for Mac, PC, and Sun SPARC systems. In the future, however, it is likely that Acrobat capabilities will be added directly to Web browsers. Netscape, in particular, has announced a deal with Adobe to do just that. This will enable you to read PDF files directly in your browser without needing an external application.

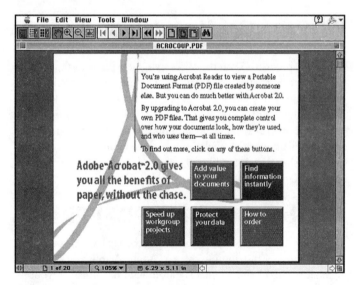

Figure 9.1. *The Adobe Acrobat reader.*

So what does PDF provide? PDF files retain all your page-based layout from the original file. For example, if you write a complex brochure in QuarkXPress with multiple columns, fonts, colors, and other nifty tidbits, converting it to HTML will lose most of that formatting (to say the least). But, using Acrobat, all you have to do is print it to PDF, and when you view the resulting file, it will look just like it did in its original form. Also, you can create hypertext links within PDF files to move from page to page, index the files, create entities similar to tables of contents, or search them for keywords. Rumor has it that future versions of Acrobat will even allow links to and from HTML pages on the Web.

Based on that information, PDF is in no way going to replace HTML. To begin with, Adobe Acrobat is a commercial package that you must purchase in order to generate PDF files. You can write HTML files for free.

Secondly, PDF files are enormous in comparison to HTML. A five-page PDF file with mostly text that I downloaded was 400 KB. A file with lots of small slides and hypertext links was 208 KB. A simply formatted version of William Shakespeare's *The Tempest* was only 195 KB for 32 pages. Of course, these files contain multiple pages, and if you combined all the HTML pages and images in your presentation, you might end up with comparable file sizes. But you can read an HTML document one page at a time. You can't (currently) do that with PDF.

Finally, PDF has no mechanism for resizing the text and layout if the screen size is larger than the page size (although you can zoom in and out). The page size is hardcoded into the file. If you're trying to read an 8-1/2 by 11 page on a small screen, you'll be doing a lot of scrolling around. And text-only browsers? Well, PDF is a display format only. I haven't currently seen any way to extract the text.

PDF is great for documents that rely on sophisticated design or page layout, such as advertisements, brochures, or very sophisticated forms. The Internal Revenue Service, for example, published its forms online in PDF format last year. For these sorts of documents—or if you really can't stand the design frustrations of working with HTML—you might want to look into Adobe's PDF as an alternative.

Where to Get More Information

You can get lots of information about Adobe Acrobat, and you can download the Acrobat reader for free, from Adobe's Web site at `http://www.adobe.com/Acrobat/Acrobat0.html`. The technical

specifications of the PDF format are published in a book from
Addison-Wesley called *The Portable Document Format Reference
Manual.*

Netscape's Dynamic Documents

In addition to the support for tables and backgrounds in the
Netscape 1.1 browser release, the capability to support the concept
of dynamic documents was included. Dynamic documents, as
defined by Netscape, are pages whose contents are dynamically
updated either as fast as possible or on a periodic basis. Uses for
this include simple animations or frequently updated information
such as stock information.

Netscape 1.1 supports dynamic documents right now, although
the mechanisms for doing so are a little tricky. The two methods
for creating dynamic documents are called *client pull* and *server
push.*

Client Pull

Client pull is the capability for the browser or client to request a
new page on its own, without input from the reader. From the
reader's end it looks like multiple pages are being loaded, one after
the other, giving the appearance of animation.

Netscape accomplishes this by taking advantage of an HTTP
header called Refresh. Refresh is sent from the server to the
browser and tells the browser to retrieve the document after a
certain number of seconds (or no seconds, to load it immediately).

So how do you get the server to send that special HTTP header?
The HTML 3.0 <META> tag provides a way to stick HTTP headers
in an HTML document. So, if you put the following line in your
HTML document, Netscape 1.1 will grab another copy of that
document after four seconds, and then another one four seconds
after that, and so on:

```
<META HTTP-EQUIV="Refresh" CONTENT=4>
```

But just having a single document refresh itself every four seconds
is pretty boring. The real fun comes when you point one page to

another, and then point that one to a third, and so on. You use a slightly different META tag for that:

```
<META HTTP-EQUIV="Refresh" CONTENT="1;
    URL=http://mysite.com/mypages/page2.html">
```

In this example, the URL is the URL of the page you want to send after this one.

Note that once you've started client pull going in the first page, your reader can't get out of it without going to a different page, closing the window entirely, or waiting until you're done. And if the browser doesn't support client pull, the reader is just stuck there on your first page. If you decide to use this in your pages, provide a way out of it by providing a prominent link to the end of the pull or to some other nonpulled page.

Server Path

The other way of doing dynamic documents in Netscape is what's called server push. Unlike client pull, in which the browser initiates multiple connections with the server repeatedly, in server push the server keeps the initial connection open and feeds multiple bits of data down to the client. You can use this to send individual documents in a series down to the client, creating roughly the same effect as in client pull. Or, you can use it to send multiple inline images to the client, with each successive image replacing the previous one in the same spot, which creates an animation inside an unchanging HTML file.

Server push relies on the special MIME type for documents called `multipart/mixed`. This MIME type is used for mail messages that contain multiple different types of data files. A program to manage multipart files of this type would know enough to handle each different bit of data in turn. Server push uses a variant of the multipart MIME type called `multipart/x-mixed-replace`, in which each different bit of data replaces the one before it.

To implement server push, you need a CGI script that outputs the right headers and then returns different bits of data at the appropriate time (which is any time you want it to). Initially, the script needs to send a `Content-type:` header of `multipart/x-mixed-replace`, with a special extra keyword indicating where the boundaries are between the different bits of data. For example, to send three HTML files successively, you separate them with a special string (it doesn't actually matter what it is), and then put that special string in the initial `Content-type` header. Here's an example:

```
Content-type: multipart/x-mixed-replace;boundary=special _string
```

With each HTML file, you include the right header and the data for the file:

```
Content-type: text/html

<HTML><HEAD>
<TITLE>The Third Document</TITLE>
...
```

Note that you don't have to send all the data at one time. Depending on how you write your CGI script, the script can do anything it wants to and then send more data when it has something to send. The client will happily sit and wait for the new data to appear while the connection is still held open.

Also, if your inline images point to a server push script that sends multiple images down the wire, you can create animations on your pages. Of course, keep in mind that the speed of the connection will have a large effect on your frame rate, but it's an interesting effect.

Server push is slightly more efficient than client pull, because it only takes up one connection as opposed to several. (Of course, that one connection is also much longer than a usual HTTP connection, so take that into account.) It's also better in terms of reader control, because simply hitting stop severs the connection and stops the flow of new data.

Where to Get More Information

Netscape's own site contains information on the specifics of developing dynamic documents at `http://home.netscape.com/assist/net_sites/dynamic_docs.html`.

You might also want to look at Home Pages' animate, a Perl script to help with server push, at `http://www.homepages.com/tools/`.

Sun's Java Language and HotJava Browser

If Netscape's clever hacks to provide dynamic document capabilities give a small glimpse into the future of Web presentations, Sun's Java and HotJava open the portal wide and suck you in. Java and HotJava are probably the neatest thing to hit the Web since... well, the Web. Intrigued? Read on.

HotJava

The HotJava browser is, at first glance, a plain old Web browser. It supports HTML 2.0 with a few of the Netscape extensions, and you can use it for browsing and filling in forms and marking pages in a hotlist just like any other Web browser.

When you encounter a page that has been written for HotJava, that's when things get interesting. All of a sudden, a little animated creature with a red nose waves at you or does cartwheels across the page. Music begins to play in the background. The headings at the top of the page swoop in from the right into position.

Or, you encounter what looks to be your basic imagemap. However, when you move the mouse over it, the hot regions highlight, and they tell you what they're pointing to in the window footer. When you move the mouse over some regions, you get a rude sound.

Perhaps you discover the game of Tetris on a Web page. Yes, Tetris. On a Web page. In real time. It works.

How is it doing all this? HotJava has the capability to download and run small applications, called *applets*, on your system. The applets are on the same page as the rest of the HTML code, in the same way that you can have inline images on a page. If you have a slow connection, the applets might take a while to load, but once they are on your system, they're quite fast. The applet runs inline with the rest of your HTML page, so you can continue to scroll and follow links and do everything you've always done in Web pages. Figure 9.2 shows the HotJava home page, as viewed in the HotJava browser. If you were viewing this in HotJava on the Web, the creature at the top of the page would be waving at you.

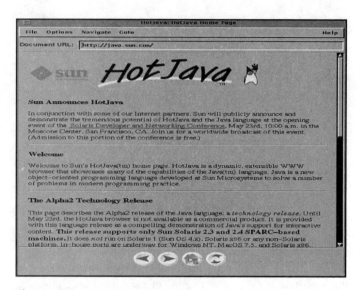

Figure 9.2. *The HotJava home page.*

But that's not all. HotJava isn't just limited to downloading applets that do cool animations and games. HotJava's capabilities extend to automatically downloading and adding whole sets of new features to the browser itself. Suppose some company offers something new on the Web—a new file format, or even an entirely new protocol for accessing files. In a normal browser, at the very least, you have to get a helper application and configure your browser to use it. In the case of a new protocol, you have to upgrade your browser. If your browser doesn't have that capability yet, you just have to wait until a new version comes out (or switch browsers). Using HotJava, attempting to access these new files or that new protocol for the first time would automatically download and install the software you need for the new format to work. It's all automatic. There ceases to be any concept of upgrading your software in the HotJava world. Neat, huh?

Java

The applets—and in fact, the browser itself—are written in a language called Java, a simple object-oriented language based on C++. Java code compiles into what are called *bytecodes*. Bytecodes are unlike a normal machine language that you get when you compile a C program, because they are fully portable across different platforms. All you need to run the bytecodes is a program called a *bytecode interpreter.* Port the interpreter, and you can run Java on your system. The core of the HotJava browser is a Java interpreter, and the capabilities of the browser, including all its networking and HTML support, are written in Java. When you visit a page with an applet on it, the browser automatically downloads the applet and runs it in the same Java interpreter. When you need a new browser capability that HotJava doesn't have, it downloads the Java to support that feature and incorporates it into the browser. It's all done for you.

But what about security? Having the capability to run applications on the reader's system would seem to be a very dangerous thing. Some nasty person might tell you to check out this cool URL using HotJava, and you might end up downloading an applet that deletes all the files on your hard drive, sends all your personal files back to the server, or just crashes your computer.

This can't happen in HotJava—or at least, it's much more difficult to do than in a normal application environment. The Java team has thought long and hard about the security of Java applets and preventing this sort of malicious behavior. First of all, the Java interpreter is self-contained. It has everything it needs to run anything without ever touching the operating system on your computer. Secondly, Java applets can't read or write from or to your hard disk without being granted explicit permission to do so (by you). Finally, the Java language, compiler, and interpreter are all designed to discourage tricks and plug up the holes that other languages might provide.

What About Other Browsers?

So what happens if you read a Java page in a browser that doesn't support Java? Nothing. HTML files with Java applets on them have a new tag, <APP>, which indicates where to find the applet and any other files it needs to run. If you're running a browser that doesn't understand Java, it just skips right over the tag. Of course, this can provide some strange looking pages, but it's not any worse than the current status of, say, tables.

Where to Get More Information

All right, you say. I'm sold. I want it. How can I get it?

Right now, Java and HotJava are only in the alpha development stage and are only available for Sun's Solaris operating system. But ports of HotJava to Windows NT, Windows 95, and the Macintosh are in the works (and might be available by the time you read this). Also, given how tremendously exciting Java is, I can say with some certainty that other browser developers will most likely incorporate the Java capabilities into their own work (although nothing has been officially announced at the moment).

You can find out all about Java and HotJava, including extensive documentation and applets you can download, from `http://java.sun.com/`.

VRML Virtual Reality Modeling Language

VRML stands for Virtual Reality Modeling Language. VRML, often pronounced *vermil* by its proponents, is a language to describe explorable multiuser 3-D spaces (or worlds) contained and distributed over the World Wide Web. VRML-based browsers use the World Wide Web mechanisms for allowing readers (explorers?) to download VRML files and render them, and VRML worlds can be linked to and from regular WWW pages. The vision of VRML is to provide a visual and perceptual interface to the World Wide Web. Instead of jumping from page to page by following links, you would wander from room to room on the Web, and encounter and interact with other explorers and objects in those worlds.

Figure 9.3 shows an example of some of the work currently being done in VRML by a group of volunteers as part of the Interactive Media Festival's VRML Arc Gallery at `http://www.arc.org/vrml/`.

Figure 9.3. *A VRML gallery.*

The VRML Language

The VRML 1.0 specification was a collaborative effort by dozens, if not hundreds, of people on the VRML mailing list, and a draft of the specification was published at the second WWW conference in the fall of 1994. VRML 1.0 allows single-user worlds with non-interactive behavior and no sound or animations; basically, it allows the creation of worlds that can be explored, but not much else. Although VRML 1.0 might seem at first glance to be somewhat limited, it does form a core set of capabilities that browser developers can work with and then build on those capabilities with VRML 1.1, 2.0, 3.0, and beyond.

VRML is based on, and is a subset of, SGI's Open Inventor file format, a popular format for describing 3-D graphics, with extensions for linking from and to normal WWW pages. VRML objects—the blocks that make up a VRML world—are called nodes and can be described on an individual basis or organized into hierarchies, with a child node inheriting rendering behavior from parent nodes. VRML defines a set of nodes that includes cubes, spheres, cones, cylinders, textures, nodes for creating groups of these objects, and nodes for creating camera angles and light sources.

Visiting and Creating VRML Worlds

To read a VRML file, you need a VRML-capable browser or a helper application that will read VRML files. VRML files have their own MIME type and extension, so stumbling across them with a regular browser without VRML capabilities will not create any odd behavior.

Template Graphics software and SGI have jointly developed the first VRML browser, called WebSpace. At this time, it is available for SGI, Solaris 2.0, AIX, Windows 3.x, and Windows NT, and it will soon be available for HP, DEC, and PowerMac. Currently, WebSpace is actually a helper application for an ordinary browser such as Netscape or Mosaic, but WebSpace can also often communicate back to the browser, allowing linked objects within VRML worlds to be retrieved and displayed as if they were linked from text pages.

Also soon available for Mac, Windows, and UNIX will be Intervista's WorldView, a stand-alone VRML browser. Intervista is noteworthy because its founder, Tony Parisi, has been instrumental in the design and development of VRML itself and was one of the authors of the original specification.

To create VRML worlds, it obviously helps to have a basic understanding of 3-D graphics concepts and a 3-D modeling tool (most of which, unfortunately, are quite expensive). Lower-end tools written specifically for VRML world development are expected soon from ParaGraph, EZ3D, Virtus, and Template Graphics.

Where to Get More Information

VRML information is everywhere! The best place to start is with the VRML FAQ at http:// www.oki.com/vrml/VRML_FAQ.html. From there, visit the original VRML Web site at http:// vrml.wired.com/, where you can get the 1.0 draft specification, source code for the VRML parser, an archive of the VRML mailing list, and pointers to lots of other sites and information.

You can get information about TGS's WebSpace from TGS's Web site at http://www.sd.tgs.com/~template/WebSpace/ index.html. Information about Intervista's WorldView is available on Intervista's Web site at http://www.hyperion.com/ intervista/.

To get involved in the development of VRML, there are several discussion lists. Check out `http://www.sdsc.edu/SDSC/Partners/vrml/repos_mailing.html` for a list of those lists and how to subscribe.

Finally, several indices of VRML information exist. One of the best is Jim Race's VRML list at `http://www.well.com/user/caferace/vrml.html`, but another good one is at `http://www.utirc.utoronto.ca/AdTech/VRML/links.html`. Also of interest are the Arc gallery pages at `http://www.arc.org/vrml/`, in which the real-life gallery and all of its contents, part of the 1995 Interactive Media Festival, will be modeled in VRML.

Creating a Secure World Wide Web

Internet security is a very hot topic these days. In particular, the capability to do secure transactions (sending credit card information securely over the Internet) for Internet shopping is of great interest to everyone involved in commerce over the Internet—vendors, customers, software developers, and Internet service providers.

Until recently, secure transactions and the secure exchange of information over the Internet has often involved either accepting the risk of transmitting sensitive data over the Net, taking the transaction off the Internet entirely (using a phone or fax machine), or encrypting the data with an encryption system such as PGP. But PGP is far too complicated for almost everyone involved and requires that you know the PGP key of the person with whom you're exchanging information. The situation with authentication has been even worse. Basic authentication in World Wide Web servers is minimally acceptable but by no means secure. Implementations of a more secure form of authentication using an encryption system have been developed, but they required modified servers and browsers and complications arose again over needing to know someone's encryption key ahead of time.

What is really needed for the World Wide Web is a general, comprehensive, and invisible encryption and authentication method between the client and the server to allow documents and information to be transmitted securely.

The good news is that there is no shortage of ideas for how to create this sort of secure environment on the Web. The bad news is that everyone's idea is different. At the moment, two proposals are vying for primary control of the Web security in the World Wide Web community: SHTTP, developed by EIT; and SSL, developed by Netscape.

SHTTP

SHTTP (Secure HTTP) is an enhanced version of the HTTP protocol that allows secure transactions in the form of signed or encrypted documents. Using SHTTP, any document you can send over the Web (HTML files, plain text, graphics files) can be securely encrypted to prevent prying eyes or data being changed. If you're interested only in encrypting the data between sites, SHTTP can be set up to accomplish that securely and invisibly. Digital signatures are slightly more complicated and require negotiation between client and server. EIT and NCSA have developed a version of Mosaic and NCSA HTTPD that includes a reference implementation of SHTTP.

SSL

SSL stands for Secure Socket Layer. It works on the premise that if you make sure the actual network connection between the browser and the server is secure and encrypted, you don't have to worry about signing or encrypting individual documents. After the data leaves the browser or the server, it is encrypted and secure. SLL is currently implemented in the Netscape Navigator browser and the Netscape Commerce Server and is available for noncommercial use as a reference implementation.

Which One Is Better?

What are the advantages of each security method? SSL is more general. Because it allows a secure network connection between the client and the server, you could theoretically use that connection for protocols other than HTTP, such as secure Telnet or Gopher. On the other hand, SSL does nothing to guarantee that the document on the server hasn't been tampered with before it even gets to the network. SHTTP guarantees not only that the information you send or receive over the wire is encrypted, but also that the document is indeed the same document that the author intended it to be.

Right now, both protocols are being trumpeted by their respective organizations as the only solution for a Web security standard. The W3 is still studying the issue and has refused to choose one side or the other. Vendors caught in the middle are hedging their bets and trying to support both, and confused users are standing by wondering whether they're going to need multiple browsers to deal with the multiple standards. (Imagine the horror of pages that say "You must be running Netscape in order to shop with us.")

Fortunately, a middle ground has been reached in the form of a company called Terisa systems (pronounced like the name *Theresa*). Terisa provides secure Web toolkits for use by browser and server developers that will support both SHTTP and SSL. It has the support of both EIT and Netscape, as well as a partnership with the major online services. Until a Web security standard is determined, using the Terisa toolkit provides a unified interface to both protocols so that users and vendors do not have to worry about competing standards (and perhaps picking the wrong one).

Where to Get More Information

For information about World Wide Web security in general, the best place to start is at the W3's security page at `http://www.w3.org/hypertext/WWW/Security/Overview.html`. That page contains pointers to companies doing general security, companies implementing digital cash, various research papers and other documents concerning Internet security, and general information about cryptography and data encryption and authentication.

EIT maintains a page of references to SHTTP, including the specification, several papers and presentations, a FAQ, and demonstrations of how secure transactions will occur using SHTTP. Find it at `http://www.eit.com/projects/s-http/`.

Netscape has produced a great reference to how SSL handles Internet security at `http://www.netscape.com/info/security-doc.html`. From there, you can get pointers to the SSL specification and information on SSLRef, the reference implementation of SSL itself.

Terisa Systems has a FAQ that describes the differences between the two protocols and why a middle-ground solution is appropriate. The company's home page also has references to the previously mentioned specifications. Terisa is at `http://www.terisa.com/`.

For more information on encryption, authentication, and security in general, Yahoo (of course) has a great index at `http://www.yahoo.com/Science/Mathematics/ServrSecurity_and_Encryption/`, including an enormous amount of information on PGP.

CHAPTER 10

By Wes Tatters

Finding It on the Web: Directories, Search Tools, and Cool and Unusual Places

Now that you have the world at your fingertips, so to speak, it's time to take a look at some of the ways that you can locate home pages and WWW sites by using the World Wide Web. Instead of creating a shopping list of popular World Wide Web sites, this chapter demonstrates ways that you can use the World Wide Web to locate interesting sites yourself.

To do this, this chapter first examines some of the major WWW directories and then looks at ways that you can search the World Wide Web and many other Internet services. Then, for those of you who really want http addresses and URLs, it briefly discusses a few of the more unique WWW pages.

Having said that, the World Wide Web is not just about pages of information provided by other people. It is also a place where you too can become a publisher. The final section of this chapter looks briefly at what you need to do to get your own home pages online and discusses, in general terms, the use of HTML.

WWW Directories

With the mind-numbing growth of the World Wide Web in the last two years, it is not surprising that more than a few people have become overwhelmed with it on their first few WWW outings. The fact that there is no front door or starting point is a concept that many people find difficult to grasp. This is to be expected, however, because our whole society is accustomed to the use of maps and step-by-step plans that always have a logical beginning and end.

For this reason, a number of WWW sites have been set up for the sole purpose of providing you with at least a logical starting point. The endpoint is still up to you, but at least these pages give you some idea about where to start.

Scott Yanoff's Special Internet Connections

The Special Internet Connections list (Figure 10.1) has been doing the rounds on the Internet in a variety of forms since 1991, when Scott Yanoff first published his personal list of Internet connections. The original list contained just six Internet sites, but since then the list has grown to contain links to thousands of World Wide Web sites, FTP servers, Telnet ports, Gophers, and mailing lists.

Since its inception, the list has been made available in a wide variety of formats, but with the growth of the World Wide Web, that version is now the most popular method of accessing the list. To explore the many links detailed in this list, use this http address: `http://www.uwm.edu/Mirror/inet.services.html`.

The list is collated by category, but not by service type. As a result, when you use this list you will often be transported to Gopher servers and FTP sites when you select a hotlink. To check the type of service that any link uses, examine the protocol section of the URL shown in the status bar when you place your cursor over its hotlink.

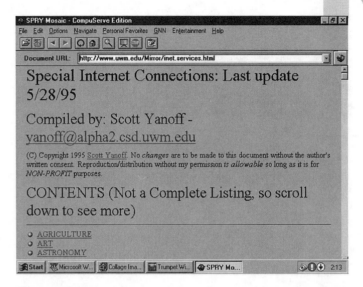

Figure 10.1. *Scott Yanoff's Special Internet Connections list includes not only WWW sites but also FTP, Telnet, and Gopher servers.*

Yahoo

Yahoo was created by David Filo and Jerry Yang, who according to *Newsweek* are two of the 50 most influential people on the Internet. They prefer to describe themselves as "Yahoos," however, and will happily direct anyone who does not know what a Yahoo is to this http address: `http://c.gp.cs.cmu.edu:5103/prog/webster?yahoo`.

Yahoo contains a comprehensive listing of popular WWW pages categorized by type. (See Figure 10.2.) The site also contains a number of unique features, including

- A What's New list, which is updated daily
- A What's Popular list, itemized by category
- David and Jerry's personal What's Cool listing
- An integrated search capability
- A random link page that takes you to a random WWW page
- The Yahoo rating system

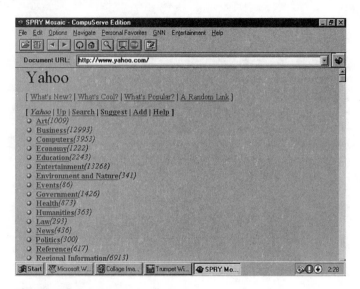

Figure 10.2. *The Yahoo WWW sites listing.*

Yahoo is provided courtesy of Netscape Communications, who provide both the server and network connections, which can be found by pointing your WWW browser to this http address: `http://www.yahoo.com/`.

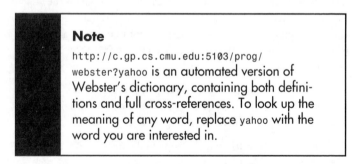

Note

`http://c.gp.cs.cmu.edu:5103/prog/ webster?yahoo` is an automated version of Webster's dictionary, containing both definitions and full cross-references. To look up the meaning of any word, replace `yahoo` with the word you are interested in.

The Whole Internet Catalog

This site is based loosely on The Whole Internet User's Guide & Catalog and contains links to all of the sites this book mentions, along with many new updates and additional references. (See Figure 10.3.)

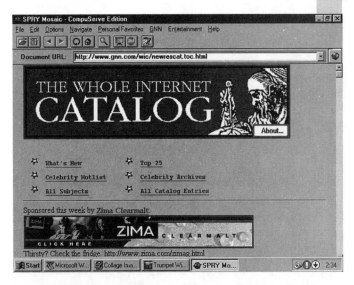

Figure 10.3. *The Whole Internet Catalog home page.*

Like Yahoo, this site contains a hierarchical list, categorized by resource type. It is not a comprehensive list; it contains only what its publishers consider to be the best WWW pages for each category listed. The advantage of this sort of list is that it helps you wade through the many thousands of pages on the World Wide Web that each tend to cover a topic in many different, though not necessarily effective, ways. This catalog reduces the number of sites you need to explore in your effort to locate information.

In addition to the general resource list, there are also special pages that cover the following topics:

- The Celebrity Hotlist, a page where special Internet guest editors are invited to share their most popular WWW pages

- The What's New listing

- The Top 25 WWW sites

The Whole Internet Catalog is provided as a part of the Global Network Navigator (GNN). To explore the links this catalog provides, use the following http address: `http://gnn.com/wic/wics/index.html`.

Global Network Navigator

The Global Network Navigator (GNN) itself, which is provided by O'Reilly and Associates, also contains links to many other popular sites and services. (See Figure 10.4.) To access this site use the following http address: `http://www.gnn.com/`.

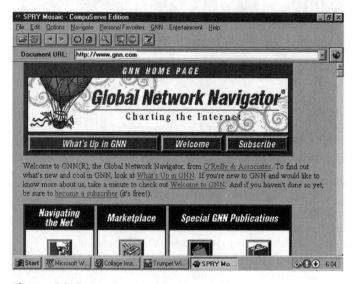

Figure 10.4. *GNN—The Global Network Navigator.*

In addition to The Whole Internet Catalog, GNN maintains a number of specialized WWW lists that include the following subjects:

- Best of the Net
- Personal finance
- Education
- Net news
- Sports
- Travel

The table of contents for GNN also provides a very good list of major WWW sites and popular home pages at `http://gnn.com/wic/wics/internet.new.html`.

> **Note**
>
> Before you can use many of the services offered by GNN, you will need to become a subscriber. There is no cost involved in doing this. All you need to do is complete the Online Information form that is available from the GNN home page by selecting the Subscribe option.

The WWW Virtual Library

By far the most comprehensive list of WWW pages currently available can be found at the WWW Virtual Library, whose http address is http://www.w3.org/hypertext/DataSources/bySubject/Overview.html. (See Figure 10.5.)

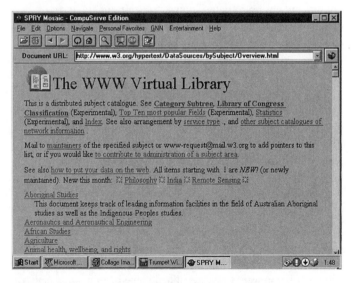

Figure 10.5. *The WWW Virtual Library contains links to most WWW pages.*

The WWW Virtual Library categorizes the pages it contains into over 150 major classifications, which themselves are often further broken down into more specific topic areas. As you may have already noticed, this service is provided by the W3 Consortium as the primary resource for WWW-related indexes. To this end, there are also a number of special pages that provide you with additional information, including

- The Category Subtree
- The Library of Congress
- Top Ten most popular fields
- The Virtual Library Index
- The Virtual Library by service type
- A list of other Internet catalogs

This site also operates in a slightly different manner than most other major lists. If someone discovers a category that is not properly represented in the Virtual Library, instead of just letting the administrators know that they have been remiss, that person often takes over the maintenance of this new area and keeps the links it contains up-to-date. To make suggestions about new categories, select the "to contribute to administration of a subject area" hotlink.

EINet Galaxy

EINet Galaxy (Figure 10.6) is organized in a slightly different manner than the other major WWW directories. At its core, Galaxy is driven by a complex database system that uses a *manufacturing automation and design engineering* (MADE) program. This program allows the categories, or information structures, Galaxy maintains to be indexed and cross-referenced in a manner not permitted by conventional hierarchical lists.

To access these indexes, Galaxy provides you with a navigation database that allows you to move easily around the Galaxy environment and quickly locate relevant information. Every information page on Galaxy contains a search field where you can enter words you want to locate. When you enter a word, a new information list is displayed that outlines all of the related information structures.

To complement the navigation database, there are also service-specific databases that allow you to search for Gopher, Telnet, and WWW links separately.

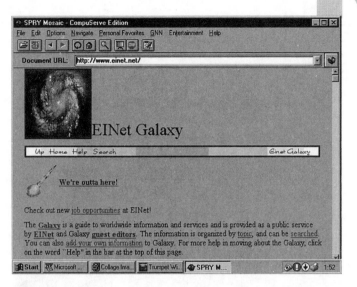

Figure 10.6. *EINet Galaxy lets you search a variety of databases for WWW pages.*

If you are interested in exploring Galaxy, you can reach it via the EINet home page at `http:/www.einet.com/`.

> **Note**
> This site also contains information about the variety of services and tools offered by EINet, which include the WinWeb WWW browser and a variety of other browser and server products.

Spry HotLand

Although far from being the most comprehensive list of WWW sites available, for Spry Mosaic users, HotLand (Figure 10.7) offers some unique capabilities.

Spry bills this page the "home of the hottest sites on the Internet." To achieve this claim, Spry professionals have spent considerable time combing the WWW looking for hot sites that offer both the best and most unique services. Although their choice of sites is still based very much on personal opinions, HotLand comes into its own because it allows you to download a copy of all of the links in each of the categories as a hotlist. Once downloaded, you can open the list as you would any other hotlist.

Figure 10.7. *HotLand WWW categories can be downloaded to your computer in the form of Spry Hotlists.*

To obtain a copy of these hotlists or to simply browse the sites Spry nominates as the hottest on the Internet, use this http address: http://www.spry.com/hotland/index.html.

The Mother-of-all BBS

For a different approach to the categorization of WWW pages, take a look at the Mother-of-all BBS listing (Figure 10.8). This site is very much a self-service directory that allows anyone to create new categories—called BBSs—and add new entries to existing ones. The http address for the Mother-of-all BBS is http://wwwmbb.cs.colorado.edu/~mcbryan/bb/summary.html.

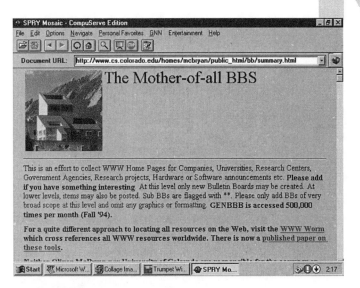

Figure 10.8. *The Mother-of-all BBS.*

WWW Search Tools

If spending hours scanning endless lists of WWW pages is not your style, maybe a more direct approach will better suit your needs.

With more than four million pages of information now directly available via the World Wide Web, not to mention the countless FTP and Gopher sites, it did not take too long for a number of WWW search tools and utilities to appear. Many of these tools provide access to a variety of information sources, including WWW pages, FTP sites or files, and WAIS directories.

This section examines some of the more popular WWW search tools and provides you with details about the types of information indexed by each.

Lycos

By all accounts, the most comprehensive index of WWW sites is maintained by a search tool developed at Carnegie Mellon

University. The name of this tool is Lycos. (See Figure 10.9.) As of the time of writing, Lycos had indexed 4.4 million WWW pages and was adding thousands of new pages each day.

Figure 10.9. *Lycos is the most comprehensive WWW index currently available.*

Like many of the WWW search tools currently available, Lycos has created its impressive index by automatically exploring the World Wide Web, page by page and link by link, following all of the paths each page offers and recording each one as it visits it. In the last six months, Lycos has become one of the busiest places on the World Wide Web, with over 15 million requests for information being answered.

To access this index, Lycos provides a variety of search options that allow you to search either the full database or a smaller "recent pages" database. There is also a simple search page and a more complex form-based page that lets you configure details such as the number of matches reported and even the search benchmarks. On the home page shown in Figure 10.9, you can choose any of these search options and select from pages that contain information about the use of Lycos. You can reach this page at
`http://www.lycos.com`.

When you type a word or combination of words into one of the
search fields provided, Lycos searches its index and displays a list
of results that match your query on a page similar to the one
shown in Figure 10.10. From here you can select any of the links
that Lycos has returned to take you directly to the WWW page
described.

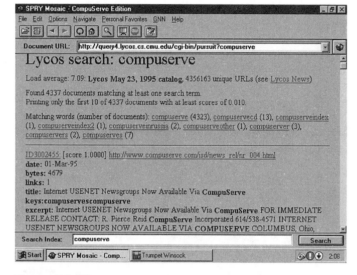

Figure 10.10. *You can select any of the links listed in the results of a
Lycos search to move straight to the nominated page.*

> **Note**
> In spite of its popularity, Lycos is still only in
> beta release. In the future, its author plans to
> include extended Boolean features and possibly
> a search capability, known as relevance
> feedback, made popular by WAIS.

Spry's Wizard

For users of Spry Mosaic, a special search tool called the Spry
Internet Wizard allows you to create hotlists based on search
results.

Like Lycos, the Internet Wizard lets you search an index consisting of WWW pages by entering a word or combination of words. Where it differs, however, is in the addition of the check box, shown in Figure 10.11, just below the search field. If you select this box, when the Internet Wizard completes its search, a hotlist is created that contains all of the links that were located. You can then download this hotlist to your local hard drive and install it on your menu in the same manner as any other hotlist you are currently using.

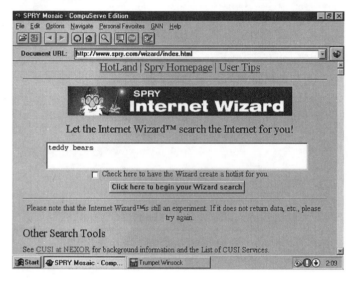

Figure 10.11. *Wizard creates downloadable hotlists based on the results of the searches it conducts.*

To access the Internet Wizard, select it on the CompuServe home page or use the following http address: http://www.spry.com/wizard/index.html.

ArchiePlex

The World Wide Web is not limited to providing WWW search tools. There are a number of other services currently available online that index many other popular Internet sources. Of these, one of the most popular is ArchiePlex.

ArchiePlex is a World Wide Web extension to the Archie. Instead of using a Telnet connection or a dedicated Archie client, by taking advantage of ArchiePlex, you can use the World Wide Web to locate files stored at anonymous FTP sites. (See Figure 10.12.) In addition, once you have located the files you are interested in (Figure 10.13), you can also take advantage of the FTP capabilities built into each WWW browser to retrieve a copy of the files and store them on your local hard drive.

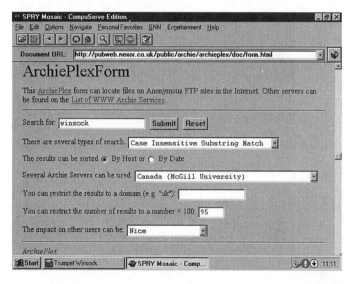

Figure 10.12. *ArchiePlex, the WWW gateway to files on FTP servers.*

There are a number of ArchiePlex pages that you can choose from, operated by WWW sites all over the Internet. To view a list of all the ArchiePlex pages currently available, point your WWW browser to http://pubweb.nexor.co.uk/public/archie/ servers.html.

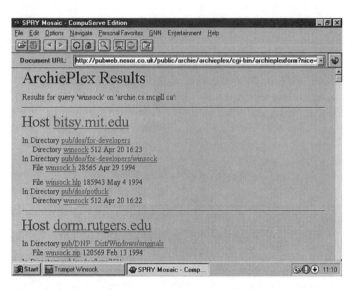

Figure 10.13. *When ArchiePlex returns the results of a search, you can simply select any of the files listed to download them.*

> **Note**
>
> Depending on the time of day, Archie servers will respond to your queries with either promptness or downright tardiness. If you find that you have not received a response within a couple of minutes, cancel the request and try another server. You do not need to change ArchiePlex pages to do this. Simply adjust the Archie server field on the request form.

WAISgate

Although most WWW browsers are capable of directly communicating with WAIS servers, the results obtained when they do are often less than suitable. To get around this problem, WAIS Inc., one of the leading WAIS publishers and developers, provides a WWW gateway called WAISgate. (See Figure 10.14.)

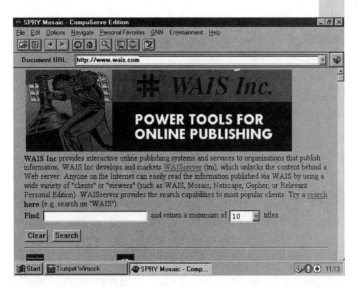

Figure 10.14. *WAISgate gives you full access to the files and databases available via WAIS.*

This gateway offers a form-based interface that greatly enhances the WWW/WAIS interface and provides a method of operation that seamlessly integrates the two services.

To access WAISgate, use the following http address: http://www.wais.com/.

> **Note**
>
> WAIS, Inc. is currently working on a new release of WAISgate dubbed WAISgate 2.0. To try a sample of what they plan to offer, select the WAISgate 2.0 demo option on the WAIS Inc. home page.

Popular WWW Search Pages and Locations

Apart from the four services already mentioned, there are about 20 other major WWW or Internet indexes and search pages, each of which offers a slightly different user interface and index. Most are not as comprehensive as those already discussed, but at the same time they often contain information that may not be available on other pages.

There are a number of ways to locate these different pages, the simplest of which is to follow the links on one of the WWW search tool pages. Figure 10.15 shows the list provided by Netscape on its WWW search page at `http://home.mcom.com/escapes/internet_search.html`.

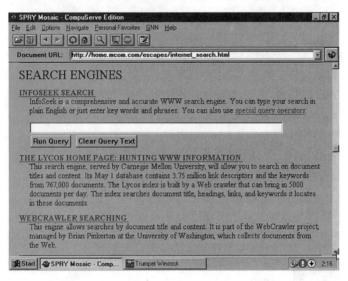

Figure 10.15. *The Netscape list of search tools and utilities.*

This page also features a direct link to the new commercial InfoSeek WWW index, which aims to provide the most comprehensive Internet index ever created.

At the bottom of this page is a link to a page known as the Configurable Unified Search Engine (CUSI). CUSI contains a list of all the known search engines that are accessible via the World Wide Web. These include:

- Lycos, WebCrawler, InfoSeek, and Jumpstation
- ALIWEB, Yahoo, Global On-Line Directory, and the CUI W3 Catalog

■ Veronica, WAIS, and the Whole Internet Catalog

■ ArchiePlex, CICA & SIMTEL Archives, HENSA Micro Archive

However, instead of just providing hotlinks to the appropriate pages, you can enter your search criterion in the space provided on the CUSI page (Figure 10.16) and click the related search button. The search page will look after the job of connecting to the search engine you selected and the submission of your query request.

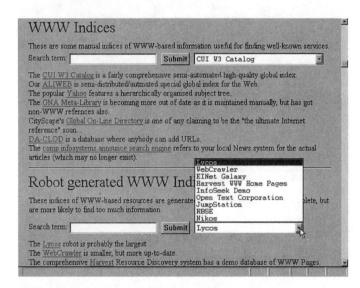

Figure 10.16. *Select the search engine you want to use and enter your query parameters. The CUSI page will look after the rest of the job for you.*

To use the CUSI interface, take a look at http:// pubweb.nexor.co.uk/public/cusi/cusi.html.

Note

Access to CUSI is also available on the Spry Internet Wizard page at http://www.spry.com/ wizard/index.html.

For a slightly different service that provides many of the same features, try `http://cuiwww.unige.ch/meta-index.html`. (See Figure 10.17.)

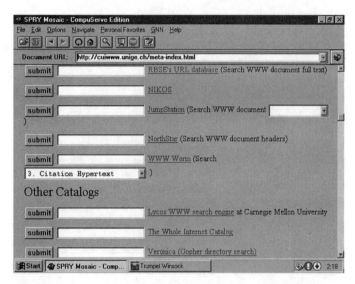

Figure 10.17. *Instead of drop-down boxes, this page lists each WWW search tool separately.*

Cool and Unusual Places

Because it seems that just about everyone else on the Internet now publishes a list of favorite places, why should I be any different? As a result, all of the WWW pages and links mentioned in this chapter are listed at my home page: `http://www.webcom.com/~taketwo/sams/nav-int-cis.html`. This is also the site of my Take Two film and television directory, among other things. (Cheap plug.)

As for the other things, in the pages that follow I have compiled a list of cool and unusual places for you to explore. This list is an ideal place to start your own exploration of the Internet and maybe even your own personal list—but more about that later. First the list: `http://www.webcom.com/~taketwo/sams/cool.html`.

GNN's Best of the Net

GNN's Best of the Net (Figure 10.18) was first proposed in 1994 as a way of recognizing expertise in all areas of World Wide Web development. The nominees for this year's awards are currently being collated here, alongside the honorees for 1995. This list recognizes not just WWW pages, but also services such as Lycos and even programs like Netscape and NCSA Mosaic that have made an outstanding contribution to the development of the World Wide Web. It can be found at `http://gnn.com/gnn/wic/best.toc.html`.

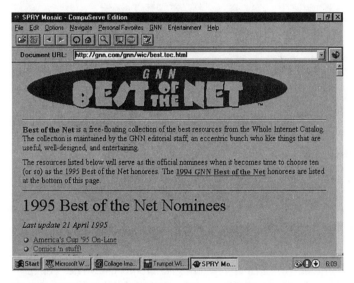

Figure 10.18. *It may not be the Academy Awards, but for Netsurfers the Best of the Net is just as important.*

> **Note**
> You might find a service that you think should be listed here; the bottom of the Best of the Net page contains instructions for making a nomination.

ESPNET SportsZone

If you're into sports, ESPNET SportsZone is the place to be. (See Figure 10.19.) Each day, the latest news and information about many popular sports and sports personalities is brought to you live via the World Wide Web. The address is `http://web1.starwave.com:80/`.

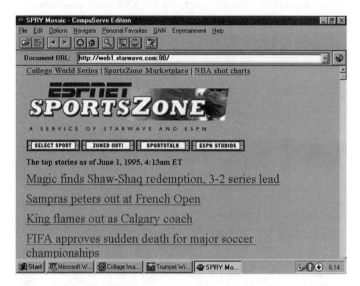

Figure 10.19. *The home of Internet sportscasting.*

You can either select from the list of sports covered, find out who's zoned out, or catch up on all the latest sports talk. When you're done, drop by the ESPN studios for all the late-breaking excitement.

The Movie Database

Have you ever found yourself in one of those arguments that seem destined to occur over coffee? Frankly, who really cares what character Clint Eastwood played in the first movie he both directed and produced? Nevertheless, it's a debate that will often drag on into the small hours of the morning. To solve this dilemma, what you really need is your handy laptop computer, a cellular modem, and the Internet Movie Database (Figure 10.20).

It can be found at either http://www.cm.cf.ac.uk/Movies/ or http://www.msstate.edu/Movies/.

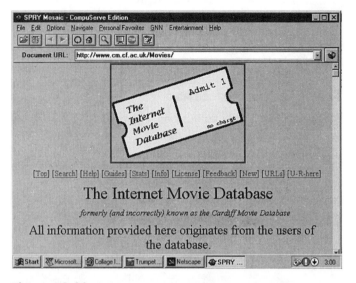

Figure 10.20. *A WWW interface to the Internet Movie Database.*

The Internet Movie Database is a classic example of what happens when a group of people with a good idea put their minds to making it happen. Since 1989, a small group of dedicated individuals have spent many thousands of hours creating what is one of the most comprehensive databases of movies, film, and television programs available today. To search this database, select the search option displayed on the home pages shown in Figure 10.20. You will be presented with a list of search options that include the following:

- Actors and actresses
- Producers, directors, and writers
- Editors, cinematographers, and costume designers
- Movie titles, release dates, and running times

Based on these parameters and many others, you can search the database and examine movie plots, cast biographies, and even lists of goofs or crazy credits.

Note

For those of you who are interested in these things, the movie was *Firefox*, made in 1982. Clint Eastwood played Mitchell Gant while both directing and producing the finished product.

The Electronic Zoo

For animal lovers, the Electronic Zoo (Figure 10.21) offers links to every related WWW page, along with a number of non-WWW sites. The Zoo was created by Dr. Ken Boschert, a veterinarian who spends many a late night surfing the Internet. It can be found at `http://netvet.wustl.edu/e-zoo.htm`.

Figure 10.21. *If it's about animals and it's on the Internet, you can find it here.*

At the Zoo, you will find sites categorized by both species and Internet service type. As a result, you can look for information by following a direct path to the animal of your choice or by a less direct, but often equally informative, path via a selection of Gopher, Telnet, mailing lists, electronic publications, and newsgroups.

To accompany this service, Dr. Ken also maintains the NetVet WWW and Gopher server, which contains information relevant to veterinary studies. The http address for NetVet is `http://netvet.wustl.edu/vet.htm`.

The White House

The White House site's biggest claim to fame is not the personal message recorded by the President or the Vice President. (See Figure 10.22.) It is not the guided tour of the White House by the First Family. Nor is it the list of publications and information about the executive branch of the United States government. Instead, it is the recording of Socks (the First Cat), which can be downloaded during the First Family tour. If you don't believe me, take a look for yourself. I won't tell you exactly where it is, but yes, it is in there.

The http address for the White House home page is `http://www.whitehouse.gov/`.

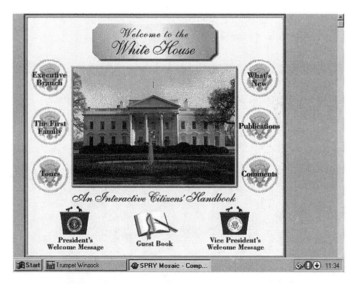

Figure 10.22. *Ever wanted to hear a personal message from the President of the United States? Click the President's Welcome Message button.*

Note

To hear any of the audio clips available on this site, your computer will need to be fitted with a suitable sound card. For those without a card, there is also a written transcript of each speech.

42—Deep Thought

If you are familiar with the four books in Douglas Adams' infamous *Hitchhiker's Guide to the Galaxy* trilogy, this page might be of interest. Basically, the trilogy is all about the number 42. I have included this offbeat page here to show that anything is possible on the World Wide Web. It's at http://www.empirenet.com/ personal/dljones/index.html (Figure 10.23).

For those of you who have not read any of the books in this series, in book two, *The Restaurant at the End of the Universe*, Arthur Dent, the book's reluctant hero, discovers that the answer to the ultimate question of Life, the Universe, and Everything is 42. The only problem is, no one knows what the question was.

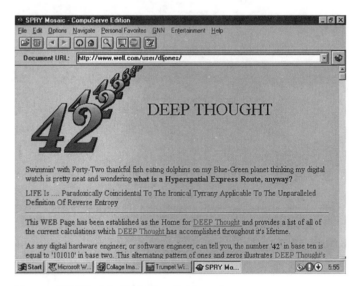

Figure 10.23. *The Hitchhikers Guide to what?*

Useless Pages, or America's Funniest Home Hypermedia

It seems to be a fact of life that the moment you turn a video camera on even the most seemingly normal person, a strange metamorphosis takes place that often results in the most astounding actions. Now it seems this same affliction is starting to appear on the World Wide Web. Give a person the ability to publish his or her own WWW page, and you often get some strange results.

And like the popular *America's Funniest Home Videos* program, there is now America's Funniest Home Hypermedia page to catalog these pages. (See Figure 10.24.) If you really want to know the contents of Scott's sock drawer, this is the page for you. This is not to say that many of these otherwise useless pages are not worth paying a visit. Some, in fact, are extremely clever and in the past have resulted in their developers receiving considerable notoriety. This page is at `http://www.primus.com/staff/paulp/` `useless.html`.

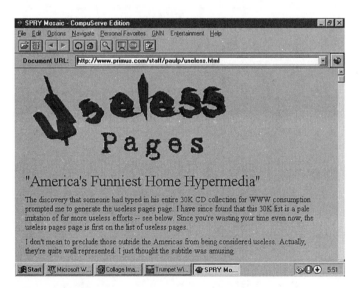

Figure 10.24. *More pages that exist because someone felt like creating them.*

Note

As a challenge, try to locate the HOTTUB page, which continually updates the temperature in Paul Haas's hot tub and refrigerator.

Understanding the Internet

To accompany their television special *Understanding the Internet*, produced in conjunction with the Discovery Channel, Cochran Interactive Inc. has created this special WWW site that provides more than 200 links to information that new Internet users will find invaluable. It's at http://www.screen.com/start (see Figure 10.25).

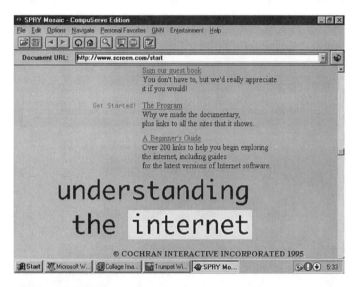

Figure 10.25. *If you want to learn more about the Internet, check out this site.*

The Macmillan Web Site of the Week

The Macmillan Publishing WWW site at www.mcp.com is the home of the Web Site of the Week competition (http://www.mcp.com/hypermail/website/). Web publishers are invited to

nominate themselves as contestants in this competition. At the
end of each week, a new WWW site is selected based on its design,
content, and overall originality. (See Figure 10.26.)

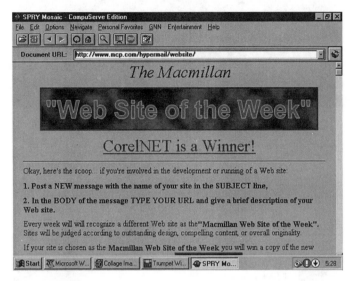

Figure 10.26. *Nominate your entrant for the Web Site of the Week
competition.*

If you have created your own WWW site and would like it to be
considered, all you need to do is follow the steps outlined on the
competition page.

WebChat

In recent months, an innovation has appeared on the Internet that
brings real-time communications like IRC to the World Wide
Web. By taking advantage of the capabilities built into many new
WWW browsers, it is now possible to use a site such as WebChat
as an interactive alternative to IRC. (See Figure 10.27.) Although
they are still very experimental, many of these chat environments
are rapidly gaining popularity as more and more people become
aware of their existence. WebChat can be found at http://
www.irsociety.com/webchat/webchat.html.

Figure 10.27. *IRC meets the World Wide Web.*

> ### Note
> To use WebChat, you need a modem that is capable of at least 9,600bps, with 14,400 or 28,800 offering better performance.

By now you should have come to the realization that with just a WWW browser you can take advantage of nearly everything the Internet has to offer. You can read newsgroups, download files, and even chat with other people in real time. By providing a single, easy-to-use interface, the World Wide Web has done more to give people access to the Internet than any other tool.

CHAPTER 11

By Suzanne Snyder,
Steve Weiss, Noel Taylor, and
Steven Vaughan-Nichols

So Where Do I Go from Here?

Now you should have a firm grasp of the World Wide Web and what it has to offer. The Web can link together information from anywhere in the world and make it available to anyone. A grade-school student can jump from Dun & Bradstreet's financial information to a pictorial tour of Croatia's capital, Zagreb, to southern Africa—without ever leaving his desk.

There's far more to the Web than just information. You can learn static facts from any encyclopedia. The information stored in the Web is constantly updated. With the Web, you'll always have the freshest information at your fingertips.

The Web also dynamically links information into a seamless whole. You may start your information hunt next door and finally track down your quarry somewhere in Singapore. From where you sit, however, the distance between the two online data sources makes no difference. The Web enables you to move around the world as easily as to the local library—with a click of a mouse.

Although the Web has existed for only a short time, it is already being used in numerous areas by both public and private institutions. Businesses have discovered how beneficial advertising and performing transactions on the Web can be. Educational institutions also are making more information available on the Web, and students are discovering that they can get increasingly more research done by searching Web pages rather than library books. You can make travel plans, buy houses, read about your favorite hobby, and make new friends via the Web.

Business

Individual companies have set up advertisements on the Web. Before long, it will be almost unprofitable for any major company—especially one that deals in new technologies—to exist without its own site to show advertisements and product information. Buyers, moreover, are rapidly finding out that it is far easier to take a look at a new product by going to a business's Web page than by physically going to the store to look for a product or searching advertisements in the newspaper. In addition to finding advertisements on the Web, consumers can do their shopping on the Web as well.

Do you want to actually purchase an item that you've been viewing? Step into a shopping mall! These malls allow users to place orders for items that can then be shipped to their homes or businesses. Holiday shopping couldn't be easier! No longer will you have to stand in lines at stores or wait on hold for the attendant at the mail-order company to take your order. Instead, you can find the item you want and have it shipped immediately.

Users can order almost anything from the Web: chocolate, books, games, clothing, music, or anything else they might desire. The directory on the accompanying CD-ROM for numerous stores and shopping centers.

Education

Many educational resources already are available through the Web. Libraries are adding their catalogs and universities are posting information about degree programs. You can also find research documents containing information about almost any subject. Before long, travelling to a library to find this information will become a near obsolete venture. Instead, students will be able to find any information sources they need without leaving their desks.

The possibilities for education on the Web are amazing. Many college and university classes presently create Web pages for semester class projects. Research papers on many different topics are also available. Even elementary school students are using the Web to access information and pass along news to other students. Exchange students can communicate with their classmates-to-be long before they actually arrive at their new school. It won't be long before students will be able to take language classes that are actually taught in the country where the language is spoken.

Many elementary and secondary schools have created and are maintaining Web pages. Students and teachers work together to decide what information should be included on the site, and to prepare it for publication. By doing this, not only do they make more information available to the community, but students gain useful knowledge of new technologies and their uses.

Travel

Planning a vacation? Many sites on the Web can help you solidify your travel plans, or give you ideas of places you might want to visit. These sites offer information about tours, and hotel accommodations, as well as car rentals, airfare, and other forms of transportation. Cruise lines have Web pages that outline various types of cruise packages and describe destinations. Many cities sponsor Web pages as well, where you can learn about restaurants, sightseeing and shopping opportunities, and local points of interest.

The Web, Controversial Content, and Freedom of Expression

The accompanying CD-ROM will show you many thousands of places to visit on the Web. There are, however, countless thousands more that aren't listed, with new sites springing up every day. The World Wide Web is a growing, dynamic, virtual world, and just like in the real world—at least in the places where unfettered freedom of expression exists—the points of view represented are myriad to the extreme. It's almost a certainty that something out there on the Web will strike you as offensive in some way.

The *Time* magazine cyberporn scare of July 1995 brought Web-content issues and freedom of expression into the national spotlight. Even though the evidence used in the report that *Time* based its story on was largely discredited, some people (few of whom seemed to be users of the Internet) began to call for government regulation of the Internet and the World Wide Web.

Everyone *Can* Use the Web

The response from actual users of the Web to this call for censorship was quick and adamant, and can be summed up as "Who do you want to decide what your kids can read, you or the government?"

In fact, before the cyberporn scare made it into the news, lots of users, content providers, and software developers were working to create means to make the Web a place for all sensibilities—without censorship.

What follows are just a couple of examples that illustrate how you can make the Web "safe" for your kids. The exclusion of other software companies or user organizations is by no means a reflection of their quality or utility.

SurfWatch Software

One of the first and highest-profile companies to address the Web "family security" issue was SurfWatch Software. The SurfWatch software you load on your computer is designed to block sexually explicit and otherwise obscene material on the Internet from being accessed by your computer (which doesn't mean it's not out there—just that your kids can't get to it).

The company has demonstrated its software before Congress in an effort to show that real alternatives to Internet censorship exist, "giving parents and educators the opportunity to limit unwanted material locally without restricting the access rights of other Internet users."

So how do they do it? Basically, the software screens your computer (while you're online) for sites likely to contain sexually explicit material. Access to unwanted sites is automatically denied. You pay $49.95 for a copy of the software, and can then purchase a subscription for $5.95 a month, which provides you with updates to the exisiting SurfWatch software (remember, several thousand new Web sites come online *each month*).

SurfWatch comes configured for Mac or Windows. You can try out the software and find out more about the company by accessing `http://www.surfwatch.com/`.

SafeSurf

SafeSurf (`http://www.safesurf.com/wave`) is a great example of Internet users working together to make the Web "safe" for kids while avoiding censorship. The folks at SafeSurf are working toward implementaion of an Internet Rating Standard using the input of "parents, providers, publishers, developers, and all the resources available on the Internet."

Ultimately, SafeSurf would like to see all "child Safe" Web sites marked with the SafeSurf Wave symbol. SafeSurf's home page explains how providers can mark their own pages with the Wave code; you can also check out SafeSurf's newsletter, lists of SafeSurf approved sites, and The Declaration of an Independent Internet.

What's especially encouraging is that companies and organizations like SurfWatch and SafeSurf are developing software that enables you to set up a computer to access a limited list of Web resources: Parents can decide not only what their kids shouldn't access; they can decide which particular Web sites their kids can visit.

About the Directory

The directory on the accompanying CD-ROM lists more than 4,800 selected World Wide Web sites. Each listing presents the site's title, and URL, as well as a brief description of the site. Many listings also contain icons that provide extra information about a site, such as whether the site is graphics-intensive or contains sound files.

The sites have been placed in category groupings, such as Children, Health, Music, Religion, and Travel, and are then presented alphabetically within those categories. Because we want to present as many sites as possible in this directory, maximum effort has been made to avoid site duplication from category to category, even if the site's contents qualifies it for more than one category. (For example, a site about church music could conceivably fall under either the Music or Religion category.)

Parts of the Directory Listings

- **Title**—The name of the site.
- **Uniform Resource Locator (URL)**—This is the "address" of the Web site. In some cases, the URL is followed by a screen shot of a graphically interesresting portion of the site.
- **Description**—This section gives you an idea of the site's contents and some of the site's outstanding features.
- **Attribute Icons**—This directory contains the following attribute icons that provide extra information about a site.

  Forms—The site contains some type of form that you can fill out if you want. Your browser may or may not have the capability to display forms. If your browser falls in the latter category, take heart. In many cases the site supplies an e-mail address so that you can contact the site's webmaster and provide him or her with the required information in lieu of filling out a form.

  Graphics—A site bearing this icon is graphics-intensive and may take a long time for your screen to display.

Netscape-enhanced—A particular site has been created and designed in such a way that it should be viewed with the latest version of Netscape. You may still view the site with an older version of Netscape or any other browser, but the site may not properly display on your screen.

Parental Guidance—This site may contain "adult" material. If you are a parent or guardian, you may wish to preview the site before allowing your child to view its contents.

Search engine— A site with this icon offers the capability to search for specific topics throughout the Web or at that particular site.

Shopping—The site offers goods or services for you to purchase if you want.

Sound—This icon alerts you that a site contains links to sound files. Because sound files take up large amounts of disk space, they may be tedious to load. Moreover, unless your hardware is configured for sound, you may not be able to listen to sound files.

Video—This site contains links to video files. Unless your hardware is configured for video, you may not be able to run these video files.

Further Reading

There are many books and articles about the World Wide Web; moreover, any relatively recent book about the Internet will contain some material on the subject of the Web. Here are some titles you might consider:

Inside the World Wide Web, New Riders Publishing

New Riders' Official World Wide Web Yellow Pages, '96 Edition

New Riders' Official Internet Yellow Pages, '96 Edition

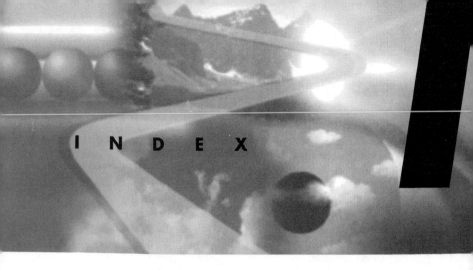

INDEX

X-Y-Z

Add to Your Sams.net Library Today
with the Best Books for Internet Technologies

ISBN	Quantity	Description of Item	Unit Cost	Total Cost
1-57521-040-1		The World Wide Web Unleashed 1996	$49.99	
1-57521-041-X		The Internet Unleashed 1996	$49.99	
1-57521-064-9		Teach Yourself Web Publishing with HTML 3.0 in a Week, Second Edition	$29.99	
1-57521-005-3		Teach Yourself More Web Publishing with HTML in a Week	$29.99	
0-672-30735-9		Teach Yourself the Internet in a Week, Second Edition	$25.00	
1-57521-004-5		The Internet Business Guide, Second Edition	$25.00	
0-672-30595-X		Education on the Internet	$25.00	
0-672-30669-7		Plug-n-Play Internet	$35.00	
1-57521-066-5		Navigating the Internet with Windows 95, Deluxe Edition	$29.99	
		Shipping and Handling: See information below.		
		TOTAL		

Shipping and Handling: $4.00 for the first book, and $1.75 for each additional book. If you need to have it NOW, we can ship product to you in 24 hours for an additional charge of approximately $18.00, and you will receive your item overnight or in two days. Overseas shipping and handling adds $2.00. Prices subject to change. Call between 9:00 a.m. and 5:00 p.m. EST for availability and pricing information on latest editions.

201 W. 103rd Street, Indianapolis, Indiana 46290

1-800-428-5331 — Orders   1-800-835-3202 — FAX
1-800-858-7674 — Customer Service

Book ISBN 1-57521-135-1